D1120790

IN THE VERNACULAR

Photography of the Everyday

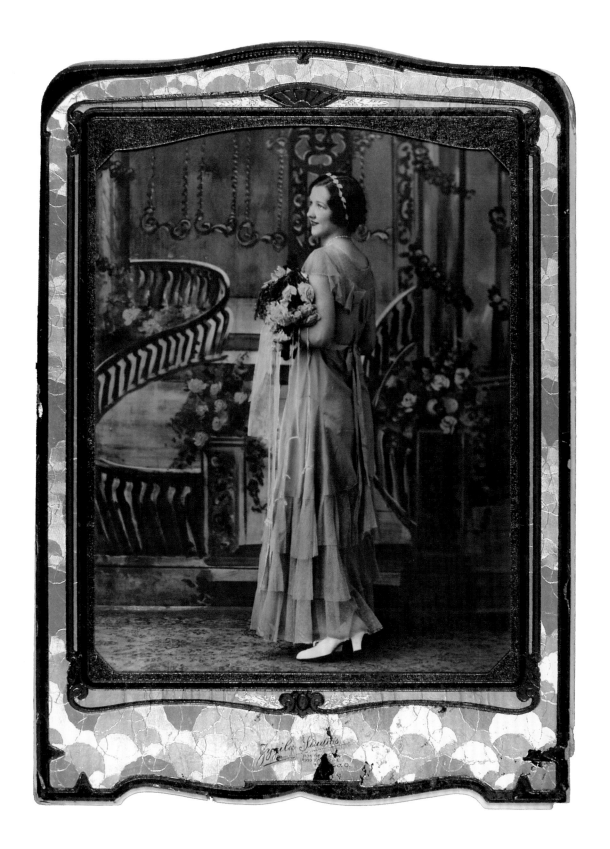

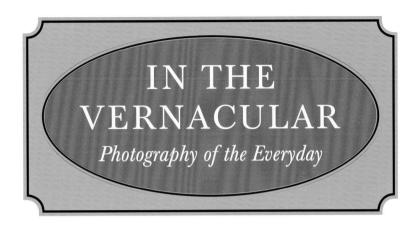

IN THE VERNACULAR
Photography of the Everyday

Stacey McCarroll Cutshaw and Ross Barrett

With essays by
Bernard L. Herman and Daile Kaplan

LIBRARY
FRANKLIN PIERCE UNIVERSITY
RINDGE, NH 03461

BOSTON UNIVERSITY ART GALLERY

2008

FRONT COVER: Anonymous
1st Grade Bruce School, W. Lynn, Mass, Nov. 1921, 1921
Contact sheet. Gelatin silver print, inscribed on verso
7⅜ x 9⁷⁄₁₆"

BACK COVER: Anonymous
Take Your Own Photos Here, c. 1950–1960
Promotional sign for photo booth with strip of four images affixed.
Gelatin silver print mounted on cardboard
13⅞ x 10¾"

FRONTISPIECE: Zygila Studios, Ohio
Portrait of a Woman, c. 1920
Gelatin silver print, hand-colored, in original decorative studio mat
9⅝ x 7⅜"

Boston University Art Gallery
855 Commonwealth Avenue
Boston, Massachusetts 02215
www.bu.edu/art

© 2008 by Trustees of Boston University
All rights reserved

"In the Vernacular: Photography of the Everyday"
© 2008 by Stacey McCarroll Cutshaw and Ross Barrett

"Vernacular Trouble: Exclusive Practices on the Margins of an Inclusive Art"
© 2008 by Bernard L. Herman

"Photography's New Identity & The Kingston Collection"
© 2008 by Daile Kaplan

All rights reserved

Distributed by University of Washington Press
P.O. Box 50096
Seattle, Washington 98145–5096
www.washington.edu/uwpress

Printed in the United States of America
Library of Congress Control Number: 2007934710
ISBN: 978-1-881450-27-6

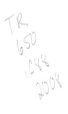

CONTENTS

PREFACE

Over the last 170 years, people have created, used, collected, and discarded photographic images in ever-increasing numbers. Despite the overwhelming presence of the photograph in daily life, until recently most types of everyday photography remained unexamined by historians and absent from the walls of galleries and museums. As photography scholars continue to study the pervasive implications of photographic production and use, the fascination of modern social life with photography in all its forms (analog or digital), and the expanding market for photographic objects, many have come to consider photography a vernacular practice. Incorporating approaches from diverse yet overlapping disciplines, including Architectural History, Art History, American Studies, Cultural Studies, Material Culture, Sociology, and Visual Culture, this study of vernacular photography has helped reshape the debate, ushering in a new phase of photographic history. This reframing served as the starting point for *In the Vernacular.*

Our particular exploration of vernacular photography began with the ideas that developed into the exhibition *In the Vernacular: Everyday Photographs from the Rodger Kingston Collection,* on view at the Boston University Art Gallery from November 5, 2004 to January 23, 2005. The exhibition was the first to highlight fully the exceptional breadth and variety of the Rodger Kingston Collection. Since the 1970s, Kingston has assembled a vast collection of visually striking images, primarily by anonymous photographers. Works from the collection have appeared in exhibitions and publications internationally since the mid-1970s. In the late 1980s, Kingston placed the bulk of the collection on deposit at the Howard Gotlieb Archival Research Center at Boston University. With access on campus to this rich and visually compelling collection of nineteenth- and twentieth-century photographs and photographic objects, I approached Ross Barrett with the proposal of collaborating on a project that considered the *idea* of vernacular photography, drawing on the collection as our visual material. The collection provided the occasion to explore some of the many functions photographs have had outside the gallery and museum.

The Kingston Collection includes over 4,000 images. In the exhibition, Ross and I created our own reading of that collection in a small sample of about 175 objects. This publication includes an even smaller selection of 70 key images. Kingston has an original and perceptive eye, as well as a keen sense of the history of photography, as his collection demonstrates. In making our selections to signify the many types of photographs at play in our everyday existence, we were able to pick particularly rich and engaging examples. The types of images and objects reproduced will be familiar to the contemporary viewer: snapshots, wedding photographs, news and advertising images, family pictures, travel albums, school portraits, pin-ups, calendars, identification badges, photo buttons, and even a photographic bandana. We endeavored to represent the diversity of modern photographic production while also demonstrating its visual appeal. Unless otherwise noted, all images in this publication are reproduced courtesy of the Rodger Kingston Collection.

Despite the possibility of misinterpretation, we purposefully chose the term vernacular for our project to generate multiple associations. Broadly speaking, "vernacular" defines that which is domestic or indigenous. In popular usage it refers to the common or everyday and can further identify the personal or private. Vernacular photography, therefore, represents the kind of photographic production that permeates daily existence. It not only includes private things such as family snapshots and photographic albums, but also includes public photographs that we might posses or encounter, such as news, advertising, or souvenir images. *In the Vernacular* frames these objects in historical and cultural contexts that encourage viewers to contemplate how photography is enmeshed in their own histories and lives. Undeterred by the growth of new technologies to capture, reproduce, and share visual images and experiences, photographs continue to serve a variety of social needs. What accounts for the longevity and persuasiveness of photographic representations? Why do we continue to hold on to photographs? What grants them power?

Ross Barrett and I organized *In the Vernacular* around four categories discussed in this publication: Archive, Proof, Surrogate, and Yardstick. These groupings highlight photographic objects in terms of their value and function. They are not meant to be mutually exclusive, and often overlap. The categories are intended as a guide and many of the images could be moved from one category to another. Our goal is to celebrate the diversity and multifarious nature of photographic production, not to read individual photographs as historical facts. Accurately identifying images by date and location, as well as interpreting content, is particularly challenging when working with many types of vernacular—and often unattributed—photographic images. We use the term "anonymous" for such unknown or unidentified makers. We provide data when available or obvious, and often made educated guesses regarding the material. Speculating on the details however can be risky as impressions are grounded in our own frame of reference. Object information and captions are intended, therefore, to elaborate on or enhance themes, and are not primarily for explanatory purposes. Again, our primary point is to focus on how photographs are used and why they are created: what needs do they fulfill? Ross, the curato-

rial team, and I generated titles, dates, and caption information. Any errors or omissions are entirely my responsibility.

I used the occasion of *In the Vernacular: Everyday Photographs from the Rodger Kingston Collection* to host a two-day interdisciplinary conference exploring the themes and ideas raised in the exhibition. Held at Boston University on November 5–6, 2004, the conference *Vernacular Reframed* brought together the foremost historians, curators, and collectors in the field to discuss questions provoked by vernacular images. Designed as a collaborative gathering, conference discussions included over 175 international participants who joined us in the audience and enhanced the experience. Sessions examined the history of vernacular photography through such topics as approaches to the vernacular, a vernacular history of photography, vernacular pictures and practices, and vernacular collectors and collections. The extensive bibliography on vernacular photography in this publication includes some sources provided after the conference by speakers and participants.

We were fortunate to assemble an accomplished and eclectic group of speakers that included curators, collectors, and historians, sometimes all in the same person, with a range of experience and expertise in vernacular studies and vernacular photography. I offer my sincerest thanks to each of our speakers for their time, energy, and collegial good will: Geoffrey Batchen, A. D. Coleman, Merry A. Foresta, Bernard L. Herman, W. M. Hunt, John Ibson, Daile Kaplan, Douglas R. Nickel, Jonathan C. Smith, Alan Trachtenberg, Stephen White, and Rodger Kingston. A gracious and easygoing group from the start, they continue to be dependable colleagues. I also thank the panel moderators for helping shape the debate: Michelle Lamunière, Melissa Renn, Jessica Sewell, and Kim Sichel. Bernard L. Herman and Daile Kaplan extended their participation by offering essays and invaluable advice on developing this publication. I thank them for their insight and commitment to vernacular photography and this project. Herman's essay provides a valuable introduction to the subject of the vernacular as a field of study, as it raises some of the thorny problems embedded in the vernacular debate. Kaplan offers an insightful overview of some key players in the early days of vernacular photographic collecting, revealing many of the issues involved in organizing and analyzing vernacular images and objects.

The 2004–2005 exhibition and conference coincided with two companion exhibitions on the Boston University campus. The Photographic Resource Center hosted the exhibition *Contemporary Vernacular*, a group show organized by Curator Leslie K. Brown, featuring contemporary responses to family and found photographs. At the time of this printing an excellent resource is active on the PRC's Web page at http://www.bu.edu/prc/vernacular/links.htm. Additionally, Boston University's Sherman Gallery sponsored *Keepsakes*, a juried student exhibition of works using or inspired by found images. Also on view was *Found Polaroids*, a collection of over 400 anonymous Polaroids presented by Jason Bitner and *FOUND Magazine*. Lynne Cooney, Exhibitions Director at Boston University's School of Visual Arts, organized the Sherman Gallery exhibitions. I am grateful to Lynne and Leslie for their contributions to the investigation of vernacular photography, which took place across the Boston University campus. With all these projects, the Boston University Art Gallery is at the forefront of vernacular photography studies, and we are thrilled at the prospect of contributing to the existing scholarship with this publication.

During my tenure as Director and Curator of the Boston University Art Gallery (2002–2007) I greatly benefited from the support and assistance of numerous friends and colleagues, both on and off campus. *In the Vernacular* has been a collaborative effort from the beginning, and there are many people to thank. First, I want to acknowledge co-curator and co-author Ross Barrett for his dedication, collegiality, and intellectual rigor. Ross has been an engaging and affable collaborator since the day we began working together. His insight, inventiveness, and breadth of historical knowledge have fueled the exhibition's growth; I have greatly enjoyed working with him. I am also incredibly grateful to Rodger Kingston, who always offered his encouragement, support, and knowledge, especially during the more difficult moments.

Conversations in my curatorial seminar in the spring of 2004 through the Art History Department at Boston University led me to new, more complex ways of looking at the vernacular and vernacular photography. I thank all the students in that course for their participation and engaging discussions. Nadia Ayari, Elise Burgess, Casey Fremont, Carly Passuite, and Rae Russell contributed lively dialogue, research, and valuable installation ideas. Following the seminar, Valerie Curtis and Jessica Nemczuk performed essential object research, as did summer intern Nadia Marx. Their research played a valuable role in the drafting of exhibition text labels, some of which appear in this publication. Julie Madden assisted with the installation process. Logen Zimmerman distinguished himself as an expert researcher early on and I took the liberty of utilizing his research skills on this and several other projects. Logen is responsible for some of the key bits of information integrated into this publication, including archival information on the Bar Harbor High School Women's Basketball Team and stereographs.

The staff of the Howard Gotlieb Archival Research Center was fundamental to exhibition development, and I gratefully acknowledge their involvement. In particular, Associate Director Sean Noel has proven an encouraging and ever-helpful colleague. Staff members Ryan Hendrickson, Nathanial Parks, J. C. Johnson, and Alexander Rankin facilitated access to and research in the collection. I also thank Director Vita Paladino and the late Howard Gotlieb for their support.

Jamie Griffith at Stanhope Framers in Boston is to be celebrated for his creative framing of the works in the 2004–2005 exhibition. I also thank him for his reliability, reassurance, and patience in working with me at BUAG over the years. I offer my fond appreciation to Vincent Marasa for his support and consistently fine exhibition design and installation work, and for his uncompromising sincerity. Additionally, Karen Haas and

9

Rebecca Senf in the photography department at the Museum of Fine Arts in Boston provided useful advice on photographic processes in relation to the exhibited works. Diane Shephard, Archivist/Librarian at the Lynn Museum and Historical Society, provided research support, as did Gary Saal, President of Pacific Licensing, and I thank them for their time.

My heartfelt appreciation goes to Paul Hoffmann, Jon Quay, John Stinehour, Dan Craven, and the entire staff of The Stinehour Press in Lunenburg, Vermont, for their goodwill and fine work on this publication. Pat Soden, Director of the University of Washington Press, graciously offered me advice on this and other publications. I extend my thanks to him and the entire staff at the University of Washington Press for our successful and congenial work together, and look forward to opportunities for continued collaborations in the future. I greatly appreciate Chris Pierson's expert editing skills. I also thank Oliver Cutshaw for providing editorial and emotional support.

The fine staff at the Boston University Art Gallery nurtured this project over the years. Marc Mitchell, Director *ad interim*, is a trusted friend and colleague and offered the freedom, resources, and funding to bring this publication to completion. I thank him for his gentle support and patience. Former Assistant Director Rebekah Pierson worked tirelessly on the exhibition and in particular on planning the accompanying conference. Her creative input and distinctive stamp still resonate throughout the project. Melissa Renn enhanced the discussion of the exhibition overall, and was essential to planning the accompanying conference. Carrie Anderson also facilitated conference-related planning. Joshua Buckno and Joshua Goode were vital to the exhibition installation process. Natania Remba, Rebecca Love, Stephanie Inagaki, and Gabriel Sosa assisted with editing text labels and exhibition installation. Lana Sloutsky provided helpful editorial assistance during book production and Leann Rittenbaum assisted with copyright research. As always, Evelyn Cohen provided support and much-needed expressions of goodwill that I have come to rely on over the years. I also thank Kaia Balcos, Ben Charland, Sarah Dillon, Maree Emberton, Molly Hopper, Samantha Kattan, Meghan Lantzy, Nilda Lopez, Karen Ann Myers, Dushko Petrovich, and Ginger Eliot Smith for their assistance.

I wish to thank Dean Virginia Sapiro and former Dean Jeffrey Henderson of the College of Arts and Sciences at Boston University for their support, as well as the Humanities Foundation and Professor Katherine T. O'Connor and Frances C. Heaton for their generous funding of this publication and the 2004–2005 interdisciplinary conference. I also appreciate the additional sponsorship provided by the Art History Department.

Kim Sichel gave me valuable insight on the introductory essay and has been a helpful colleague and mentor throughout this project. I want to thank additional friends and colleagues affiliated with Boston University who have supported and sustained me over the years: Kate Palmer Albers, Virginia Anderson, Catherine Blais, Rachelle Dermer, Michèle Furst, Jaimey Hamilton, Lawrence Hyman, Stephanie Mayer Heydt, Louisa Iarocci, Michelle Lamunière, Chris Newth, Caroline Jones, Patricia Hills, and John Stomberg.

STACEY McCARROLL CUTSHAW

IN THE VERNACULAR:

PHOTOGRAPHY OF THE EVERYDAY

Stacey McCarroll Cutshaw and Ross Barrett

The Rodger Kingston Collection includes an untitled photograph of a man posing with a bear in a forest clearing [page 56]. Like many objects in the collection, this photograph is unsigned and undated. It carries no informative inscriptions or markings, and the scene includes no telling spatial or temporal landmarks. The unmarked photograph is literally and historically unframed, now an image disconnected from the physical, social, and symbolic structures that set its meaning for its original viewers. The contemporary viewer has only the visual content of the photograph to consider and analyze: a rather ordinary man, styling himself as a hunter, poses with a rifle and a dead black bear hung by the jaw on a hook.

In its apparent muteness and anonymity, the hunter photograph suggests the difficulties facing the historian, critic, or curator who seeks to interpret and historicize vernacular photographs, the everyday images and objects that, as Geoffrey Batchen has noted, have constituted the overwhelming bulk of photographic production since its inception.[1] Often the handiwork of now anonymous picture-makers and the result of spontaneous processes, vernacular photographs refuse to be organized or analyzed according to the paradigms that have guided traditional historical studies of photography, such as authorial intention, artistic expression, originality, and formal innovation. As a result, vernacular photography was long relegated to the margins of photographic history, a history that has occupied itself with photography's fine-art status

and so has focused primarily on the self-consciously aesthetic productions of artistic photographers.

The exhibition *In the Vernacular: Everyday Photographs from the Rodger Kingston Collection* mapped out a different approach to vernacular photography. Moving beyond the aesthetic surface of the photographic image, the exhibition highlighted the many ways photographs are used in our daily lives. Driven by the rich visual material of the Kingston Collection, we organized photographic images and objects into four categories: Archive, Proof, Surrogate, and Yardstick. Describing some of the everyday functions that photography has performed over its history, these categories foreground the material and social lives of photographic images and objects. After a brief introduction to the historiography and bibliography of vernacular photography—key texts that shaped our thinking on the subject—this essay returns to the four categories and the images that guided their construction, presenting a fresh approach to the study of everyday photography.

In the last decades of the twentieth century, critics and historians began to question the high-art focus of photographic history, and to explore more comprehensive approaches to the study of photography. Historian John Kouwenhoven initiated these investigations in a 1972 lecture, announcing that we were "living in a snapshot world." Kouwenhoven presented an analysis of photography that not only considered aesthetics, but also the social, cultural, and technological histories of the ubiquitous snapshot image, a photographic form that, in his argument, had ushered in a new visual language and altered our sense of history.[2] In 1992, American critic A. D. Coleman and British cultural studies scholar Dave Kenyon built on Kouwenhoven's earlier work, arguing separately for a new mode of historical study that could account for the full spectrum of photographic production and the many forms of photographic practice employed in the Western world (and elsewhere). In an article titled "Quotidian or vernacular photography," Coleman declares:

> However, we are in a period of radical revisionism in regard to photography's history, and the time is proving to be ripe for challenges to these attitudes—especially since they embody a variety of prejudices and oversights. For if there is indeed one truth that must underlie any future unified field theory of the histories of photography, it is that those histories include all the photographs ever made, as well as all of the people who produced them, who are represented in them, and who laid eyes on them.[3]

Coleman's unconditionally inclusive call to "include all the photographs ever made," is daunting but also conceptually promising. In order to meet these needs, he argues for a "sociology of photography," based on models articulated in the work of historians such as Mary Warner Marien, Bill Jay, and Gisèle Freund, that can account for the totality of photographic production, as well as the "conditions of creation" for every image produced.[4] Correspondingly, Kenyon takes an interdisciplinary approach to photography, championing terms such as "amateur," "popular," "everyday," and "domestic" in his book, *Inside Amateur Photography*. As Kenyon describes, "vernacular photography is the shared picture language of ordinary people," a language that allows for the exploration of "personal experience through picturing."[5] In their separate studies, Coleman and Kenyon call for the reinvigoration of photographic history through the study of previously unseen and unstudied groups of images and image-makers, the everyday objects and producers of vernacular photography.

As art historian Elizabeth Hutchinson has noted, many of these early photographic studies drew on the work of architectural historians and material culture scholars, who first developed the category of the "vernacular" to organize and analyze objects and buildings made outside of, and even in opposition to, elite culture.[6] Frequently cited scholars in this context include Dell Upton, John Michael Vlach, Thomas Carter, Bernard L. Herman, and Jules Prown.[7] Many initial vernacular photography studies also utilized interpretations of everyday photographs by prominent sociologists, cultural critics, and semioticians, including works by Pierre Bourdieu, Susan Sontag, and Roland Barthes.[8] Incorporating this range of methods allowed for both *practical* and *theoretical* approaches to the study of vernacular photography.

Several exhibitions organized around the commemoration of photography's sesquicentennial in the late 1980s extended scholarly efforts to rethink photographic history by surveying a more complete account of photographic practice, moving away from the great-masters-of-the-medium model and including anonymous or non-high-art photographs. For example, Sandra S. Phillips's first major effort as Curator of Photography at the San Francisco Museum of Modern Art, "A History of Photography from California Collections" (February–April 1989), was organized to launch a four-part series celebrating the 150th anniversary of the invention of photography. This unusual exhibition not only focused on the local example of California (exhibiting materials borrowed from archives and historical collections), but also included anonymous images from the nineteenth and twentieth centuries.[9] At about the same time, Daile Kaplan organized a notable exhibition, *150 Years of Pop Photographica*, for the Islip Art Museum on Long Island, New York (December 1988–January 1989), which illuminated the relationship between photography and popular culture and resurrected an array of everyday photo-objects for historical study. With these exhibitions, Phillips and Kaplan asserted the importance of vernacular photographs as objects of cultural history, and shed new light on the exclusion of vernacular images from established photographic histories.

Beginning in the late 1990s and early 2000s, a concerted effort to address the omissions of photographic history emerged through intense curatorial and scholarly investigations of vernacular photography. In 1997, Geoffrey Batchen organized the exhibition, *Photography's Objects*, for the University of New Mexico Art Museum. The following year, Douglas R. Nickel organized *Snapshots: The Photography of Everyday Life, 1888 to the Present*, for the San Francisco Museum of Modern Art. Exhibition catalogues that addressed the historical, theoretical, and interpretive problems posed by vernacular photographs accompanied both exhibitions.[10] These influential projects outlined different approaches to everyday photographs (described later in this essay) and prefigured a succession of later, significant exhibitions of vernacular photographs, photo-objects, and collections, including *Other Pictures: Vernacular Photographs from the Thomas Walter Collection* at the Metropolitan Museum of Art (2000), *The Photograph and the American Dream 1840–1940* at the Van Gogh Museum in Amsterdam (2001–2002), the expanded and reorganized *Pop Photographica: Photography's Objects in Everyday Life, 1842–1969* at Toronto's Art Gallery of Ontario (2003), *African American Vernacular Photography: Selections from the Daniel Cowin Collection* at the International Center of Photography (2005), *The Art of the American Snapshot, 1888–1978: From the Collection of Robert E. Jackson* (2007) at the National Gallery of Art, and our own Boston University Art Gallery exhibition in 2004–2005.[11]

Alongside these exhibitions, a stream of books devoted to specific types of vernacular photographs started to appear, such as John Ibson's *Picturing Men: A Century of Male Relationships in Everyday American Photography* (2002), *Least Wanted: A Century of American Mugshots* by Mark Michaelson and Steven Kasher (2006), and *Real Photo Postcard Guide: The People's Photography* by Robert Bogdan and Todd Weseloh (2006).[12] This surge in exhibitions and publications suggests the new significance of vernacular photography as a focal point for studies of photographic practice in the twenty-first century. Indeed, scholars and curators have begun to pursue a range of new ideas about vernacular photography, its place in the history of the medium, and the analytical approaches best suited to its diverse and challenging pictures and practices. While some of these endeavors have taken more traditional paths—exploring, for example, the "accidental" formal connections of amateur and anonymous images to canonical art photography—most were undertaken with an interest in moving beyond hierarchical, formalist models of photographic history and the limited artistic canon those models have labored to construct. In his 2000 essay "Vernacular Photographies," for example, Geoffrey Batchen argues, "expanding the canon of course has its momentary value, but what is needed here is a rethinking of the whole value system that canonization represents. . . . So we are already talking about developing a history that contests traditional boundaries and disturbs existing oppositional structures." Building on this idea of an alternative historiography, Batchen has suggested that this new approach might in fact require multiple interpretive modes suited to the heterogeneous character of the wide field of vernacular production.[13]

Batchen outlined this argument in a special issue of *History of Photography* that appeared in the fall of 2000. Devoted to the problem of the vernacular, the essays included in the journal rearticulated, and began to answer, recent calls for a dynamic and shifting approach to the historical study of everyday photography. As guest editor, Batchen introduced the discussion with a synopsis of attitudes toward the very term "vernacular photography" from historians, collectors, and curators including Hutchinson, Kaplan, Nickel, William Hunt, Elizabeth Edwards, and André Gunthert. This group's responses to a set of questions posed by Batchen offered a de facto "state of the research" account of vernacular photographic history. The varying opinions and lack of agreement on the very utility of vernacular photography as an explanatory framework demonstrate both the possibilities of the field and some potential perils of indistinct disciplinary boundaries.[14]

For Nickel, vernacular is "a kind of non-category," the residue or remainder of the photographic art history established in the early twentieth century by figures such as Beaumont Newhall and Helmut Gernsheim:

> Since this wasn't a social history of photography—which is to say a history of photographic practices—one finds a funny ambivalence towards such notions as photography as a technology, photography as commerce, or photography as a popular amateur medium. The net result is that we've inherited a bipartite model from these earlier histories—'art' photography, and everything else. If a photograph wasn't made for non-utilitarian, self-consciously expressive reasons that allow it to be designated 'art', it devolves to this grab-bag left-over category designated 'vernacular'. Vernacular is thus defined not by what it is, but what it isn't.[15]

Gallery Director and collector William Hunt wondered why *vernacular*, when used with "photography," is often set in quotation marks—something we have avoided in this publication—as if to demonstrate the hesitancy of the categorization. For Hunt, "a vernacular (why the quotation marks?) photograph is any photograph made without any art-historical considerations. The term connotes populist origins, family or scientific documentation." Accordingly, Hunt argues, "Most vernacular work is not artistic, nor is it intended to be timeless."[16] Visual anthropologist and curator Elizabeth Edwards argued for culturally specific vernacular photographies. She explained,

> I have big problems with some vernacular photographs being shown in 'art' contexts, especially cross-culturally where there is a tendency to collapse everything into neo-exoticism . . . Also there is a tendency to absorb them into the established discourses rather than explore what is culturally specific and relevant about this particular body of work . . . I would like to see more 'ethnographies of photography' happening which would look at what is specific about certain forms of practice.[17]

While multiple interpretive strategies have been proposed for the study of vernacular photography, two basic, divergent modes of analysis have come to define the scholarly and curatorial efforts of the moment: one focused on recovering the original conditions of vernacular photographs' social use, and the other on interpreting the meanings everyday images acquire *after* their initial production and consumption. Elizabeth Hutchinson laid the foundations for the first of the prevailing methods, suggesting "perhaps the best solution is to move away from an emphasis on what photographs look like to how they are used."[18] Edwards developed this concept, arguing that "vernacular photography encompasses a wide range of photographic practices where the aesthetic or expressive considerations of image making are secondary to their functional uses, both in terms of image content and in the social use made of those photographs."[19] Together, Hutchinson and Edwards suggest an historical approach to the ordinary photograph that emphasizes and reconstructs the social function of that image or object in its original context. Taking up this method, subsequent scholars have emphasized the social function and initial historical context of vernacular photographs, analyzing images for their everyday use-value.

In his compelling essay "Vernacular Photographies," included in the *History of Photography* special issue, Batchen accordingly suggests the importance of the "morphological" dimensions of everyday photographic use and experience.[20] Invoking methodological precedents from the work of Jacques Derrida and Roland Barthes, Batchen examines photographs produced in the domestic sphere, emphasizing the physical experience of the photographic object, particularly the sense of touch. In subsequent works, including his 2004 exhibition and publication *Forget Me Not: Photography & Remembrance*, Batchen has continued to develop this objective, closely analyzing the physicality of the photographic object. In so doing, he has attempted to "make photography the visual equivalent of smell and taste, something you can feel as well as see."[21] Photography critics and historians have taken up and extended Batchen's morphological approach in a variety of studies, including the 2004 volume, *Photographs Objects Histories*, edited by Edwards and Janice Hart. The essays in this stimulating and dense publication take an international approach and emphasize the centrality of the photograph's "objectness" to analyses and comprehension.[22]

Other scholars, Nickel foremost among them, have endorsed an approach that emphasizes the contemporary experience of the vernacular image and traces the lives of photographs after their initial production and consumption. Nickel proposes the basic outline for this methodology in his 1998 catalogue essay on snapshots in *Snapshots: The Photography of Everyday Life, 1888 to the Present*, noting:

> When the snapshot becomes 'anonymous'—when the family history ends and the album surfaces at a flea market, photographic fair, or historical society—and the image is severed from its original, private function, it also becomes open, available to a range of readings wider than those associated with its conception.[23]

Disconnected from its original familial circuits, the anonymous snapshot "becomes open" to new interpretations and new meanings forged by the "active, creative imagination" of the viewer. Drawing on poststructural theories of "open" or "readerly" texts and the tenets of reception theory, which asserts the importance of the reader in the construction of meaning, Nickel emphasizes the ways anonymous snapshots ask the contemporary viewer to complete them as symbolic productions. "The snapshot, like other photographs, suffers an excess of potential meaning, but when removed from conditions that normally limit its polysemous nature, it may offer itself to the pleasure of our active, creative imaginations. Like haiku, it will ask us to complete it."[24] Interacting with the image, the viewer enters the "terrain . . . of affect," exploring the emotions and sentiments that accompany the experience of photographs that are both familiar and mysterious.[25] For Nickel, attentiveness to the "affective relationship between object and viewer" represents a fresh approach to the interpretation of vernacular photographs, one capable of addressing a broader range of everyday images and objects.[26]

In centering his analytic approach on the snapshot's "power over us," its affective force for a contemporary audience removed from its original function, Nickel aims to avoid the pitfalls of canon formation and the imposition of an aesthetic imperative on ordinary photographs.[27] Despite the efforts of Nickel and others to advocate innovative approaches that avoid traditional structures of canonicity and judgments about aesthetic quality, however, vernacular projects continue to take a variety of customary and experimental tacks in addressing the everyday image. Take, for example, two recent projects that fall under the rubric of the snapshot: the 2007 National Gallery of Art exhibition and publication *The Art of the American Snapshot* and the 2005 exhibition and publication *Snapshot Chronicles: Inventing the American Photo Album* at Reed College's Douglas F. Cooley Memorial Art Gallery.[28] The very title of the National Gallery project demonstrates that the intention is to present snapshots as *art*, with an impulse toward the aesthetic as the basis for the exhibition. The exhibition's content, moreover, seemed to bear out an underlying aesthetic imperative. Proposing to examine the ways in which "changes in culture and technology" have "enabled and determined the look of snapshots," and thus to pursue a contextualizing approach, the show nevertheless focused on photographic "looks" or visual themes (such as doubling, ironic juxtapositions, aggressive cropping, and strategic ambiguity) that resonate with the formal experiments of modernist artistic photography, experiments that have guided past treatments of vernacular images as works of anonymous aesthetic "genius."[29] The critical risk here is that images that do not measure up to some standard of visual interest—images that center their subjects, that emphasize stasis rather than dynamism, or that disclose visual information straightforwardly, for example—can be easily overlooked. Despite the exhibition's uneasy resolution of aesthetic and historical approaches to photographic interpretation, the immense publication accompanying *The Art of the American Snapshot* is rich in scholarly content, featuring comprehensive historical essays by the curatorial team. If the National Gallery exhibition subtly reasserted the aesthetic effects joining snapshots and fine art photography, the Reed College project presents snapshots in a more conventionally historicist frame, focusing on examples of the family photo album. The well-designed publication accompanying the exhibition presents a wealth of examples, reproduced in such a way as to give a sense of their physical presence. This project looks at snapshots in their original symbolic and material context and begins to address the serious lack of historical or scholarly work done on the photographic album.[30] Although the short essays included in the book approach the material from different perspectives—collecting, curatorial, and literary—its contribution to the scholarship is modest.

*   *   *

In the Vernacular: Everyday Photographs from the Rodger Kingston Collection was organized in the midst of these reexaminations of vernacular photography, and as such endeavored to engage with the arguments, questions, and problems raised by recent photography historians, collectors, and curators. The exhibition was especially concerned with the call for a new form of history, a vernacular history, that could account for everyday photographic images without reference to traditional historical narratives (the progress of formal development), thematic emphases (intentionality and originality), or the need to confine images to specific visual tropes (images of clowns, cats, athletes, etc.). As a preliminary and experimental step toward such a vernacular form of photographic history, *In the Vernacular* arranged 175 photographs and photographic objects drawn from the Kingston Collection, and representing the nineteenth and twentieth centuries, according to four broad and overlapping groupings related to the social function of everyday photographs: Archive, Proof, Surrogate, and Yardstick. These contextual groupings were intended to address the ways photographs work in our daily lives, and how we work with them. In emphasizing the functionality of everyday photographs, the exhibition followed the precedents suggested by Batchen, Hutchinson, Edwards, and other photographic scholars. At the same time, however, the groupings were chosen for their fluidity and expansiveness, for their capacity to

account for a range of photographic objects from a variety of periods, and for the changing and dynamic uses of these objects during and after their initial socio-historical context. In however provisional a fashion, *In the Vernacular* attempted to bridge some of the diverse approaches that have been brought to bear on vernacular photographs.

The four categories proposed for *In the Vernacular* (Archive, Proof, Surrogate, Yardstick) correspond to some of the most basic and enduring uses made of photography since its inception. Not merely contextual, these historical and socially determined categories also describe deep formal conventions and structures. Indeed, the categories were formulated with the idea that the visual and material forms of vernacular objects bear traces and symbolic projections—often subtle or complex—of their eventual social functions, formal clues that are open to analysis and interpretive recovery. Curators and historians have since elaborated on the notion of a formal or visual inscription of use-value. As Brian Wallis recently argued:

> Yet, these images conform to a strict and highly codified set of rules that determine the appropriate poses and rituals to photograph. The repetition of these conventions—which are different but equally important for wedding photographs or passport photos—allow the images to be read properly by the designated viewer. In this sense, vernacular photographs are defined more by their destination than their origin.[31]

Echoing Wallis, we proposed that the visual content of ordinary photographs—their settings, compositions, uses of focus, figural poses, emphases and elisions—can often communicate the fundamental social functions of these often anonymous and unnamed objects.

With the anonymous object in mind, we might return to the seemingly cryptic photograph of the *Hunter with Bear* (c. 1920s) [page 56]. Gripping a Winchester rifle somewhat woodenly in one hand, the mustachioed man holds the limp paw of a dead black bear that hangs beside him. The poses of man and animal are strangely similar. Both are pictured in identically full-figure, "standing" positions. Both seem to take

16

a wide stance. Both turn slightly inward, toward the other; and both extend their arms slightly away from their torsos, with the outside arm hovering over the outside leg, and the inside arm reaching for the other figure. The composition thus takes shape around two meaningful visual themes—intimacy and exact correspondence—that in turn seem to point to the function of this anonymous image. On the one hand, the strange mirroring of hunter and bear invokes conventional notions of photography's exact fidelity as a representational system and its technological command over the natural world (its capacity to "freeze" nature in static portraits), notions likely shared by the original maker of the image.

As Batchen has noted, vernacular objects frequently bear this sort of self-reflexive engagement with the indexicality ascribed to photography.[32] In the photograph at hand, this engagement seems to affirm a particular reading of the image (perhaps with some measure of anxiety): the exact correspondence of man and animal suggested to the period viewer that he or she was looking at an equally faithful double, or record, of the moment depicted. But what exactly was recorded? Arranged near the center of the photograph, the strangely affectionate hand-and-paw embrace asserts the fundamental importance of closeness or intimacy to the scene. Like many modern "trophy" photographs, the anonymous image above all testifies to the daring intimacy with wild nature experienced during the hunt, offering its viewer a document proving the closeness with unpredictability and chaos enjoyed by the rather less-than-heroic-looking, bourgeois hunter.

The hunter photograph points us in turn to a basic function that might be ascribed to a wide range of photography in a variety of historical moments: the offering of *proof*. Drawing on faith in the veracity and mimetic truthfulness of photography, people have long turned to photographs for proof or evidence: for ostensibly objective confirmations of dubious beliefs and contentious claims, for private and official validations of experience and memory, and for authentications of stunning, ambiguous, and otherwise inaccessible phenom-

ena. Invoking this traditional photographic function, Roland Barthes noted, "the important thing is that the photograph possesses an evidential force . . . in the Photograph, the power of authentication exceeds the power of representation." Like Barthes, many photographic viewers find it difficult to "deny that *the thing has been there*," no matter the extent or accuracy of their reading of that thing itself.[33]

Drawing on pre-photographic traditions of painted marriage portraits, wedding photographs have long offered another form of proof, serving as official visual documents of matrimony since the nineteenth century. *Wedding C. M. Henry & E. A. Dohrman* (c. 1890) [page 60], an albumen print mounted on cardboard and inscribed, records a late-nineteenth-century wedding party. The groom and bride are pictured at far left; the minister is in the center with two male witnesses at far right. As an added level of verification, someone has handwritten the names of each participant just below their images, confirming their collective participation in this important event. In this instance, the visual information provided in the photograph is augmented with explanatory text. We do not know who inscribed the image or when the names were added. As with many family photographs, it is possible another family member—someone not represented in the scene—added the names later in order to insure that this information, and a more complete reading of the scene depicted, was not lost to posterity.

Produced sometime in the late nineteenth century, *Wedding C. M. Henry & E. A. Dohrman* registers the growing importance of photography to private and public rituals, its progressively more pivotal role in shaping, and even defining, social experience. As Susan Stewart has argued in her book, *On Longing: Narratives of the Miniature, the Gigantic, the Souvenir, the Collection*, wedding photographs would come, by the mid-twentieth century, to occupy center stage in the ceremonies of matrimony: by the 1950s, she argues, "the traditional wedding had fully moved into its contemporary status as a photographic, rather than primarily social, event, the reception of guests being eclipsed by the photography session." As such, Stewart continues, "The event in itself is like the photograph—a depiction of an event effected through a reduction of physical dimensions, a picture which becomes both the occasion for the event and a replacement for it."[34] Carefully detailing the setting and participants of a turn-of-the-century wedding ceremony, *Wedding C. M. Henry & E. A. Dohrman* prefigures the photographic weddings of midcentury, offering visual proof of a fleeting social event.

Photographs and photographic objects are also used to authenticate and verify a range of less tangible phenomena and beliefs. *In the Battle for Democracy, Justice, Humanity* (1918) [page 59] is an elaborate photo-object, combining a small gelatin silver print of an American soldier during World War I with a colorful, mass-printed poster embellished with a giant, rippling American flag, a bald eagle, a stand of Allied flags, and two scenes of warfare in the background. Carefully inscribed "Corporal Augustus G. Roycroft, 322nd Infantry, 81st Division," the photograph at center depicts the non-commissioned officer leaning against a prop table in a photographer's studio. Born in 1892 to John and Martha Roycroft in Granville County, North Carolina, Augustus Roycroft was an unmarried farmer when he enlisted in 1917 as part of the American Expeditionary Force.[35] Organized primarily of Southern draftees in August of 1917, the 81st Division was first stationed at Camp Jackson, South Carolina, before leaving for France in July 1918. Roycroft's division participated in the Meuse-Argonne Offensive, the largest U.S. engagement and one of the most deadly. Flanked by fanciful images including a steaming destroyer accompanied by whimsical biplanes, an artillery crew bravely blasting away at unseen targets, and a host of national symbols, the humble farmer is firmly enmeshed in an idealized vision of the Allied war project. In this way, the total photo-object offered Roycroft's friends and family reassuringly compelling proof of his role in a war effort that was, while international and necessarily abstract, nevertheless virtuous, patriotic, and well designed.

Other vernacular objects enact more ambiguous displays of photographic proof. *Woman with Fish* [page 51], for example, employs specific visual codes associated with verification, yet the photograph's message remains uncertain. The visual organization of the scene, which probably dates from the 1950s, replicates standard conventions of hunting and fishing imagery: a smiling woman stands next to a large tuna that hangs vertically from a support just outside of the top of the frame. Echoing the pose in *Hunter with Bear*, the woman touches the dorsal fin of the fish in a caressing gesture that again suggests an intimacy or closeness with wild nature. Tuna of this species are a popular game fish, and were often the targets of deep-sea sport fishing tournaments prevalent in the United States in the 1950s and 1960s. It is possible that the woman depicted caught this trophy fish herself, yet the cleanliness of her outfit—pressed wool pants and a snappy blazer unblemished by blood or toil—compel us to question the likelihood that she alone reeled in the large fish. She may have been a participant or bystander in the fishing party, or perhaps performs here as a visual measure, demonstrating the tremendous size of the catch. Or the woman might have taken on the role of the triumphant fisherwoman to humorously undermine the authenticating capability attributed to photography. Whether responsible for the catch or not, she performs for the camera according to the rules of the typical trophy image. As viewers and interpreters, we must approach *Woman with Fish* with skepticism, aware of the limitations of photography's representational verisimilitude. Perhaps not proof of her personal "great catch," the photograph certainly documents a good day and reminds viewers to question the codes enacted in and assumptions of all photographic imagery.

Other photographic objects in the exhibition similarly thematize the untrustworthiness of photographic images. Like most of the police documents inspired by the work of French criminologist Alphonse Bertillon, the 1908 photo-cards *Albert Johnson* and *Edward Cooper* supplement their visual information with extensive textual notations [page 50]. Intent on generating maximally accurate and conclusive records of criminal behavior, Bertillon devised a detailed system of documentation that combined photographic portraits of arrested offenders with lists of their physiological and anthropometric measurements. Bertillon combined these divergent systems of representation on standardized cards that could be organized in file cabinets. As Allan Sekula has argued in his decisive article, "The Body and the Archive," these cards enmeshed photography in broader systems of information, systems premised on a new awareness of the insufficiency of the photograph as a self-contained, authoritative document:

> Contrary to the commonplace understanding of the 'mug shot' as the very exemplar of a powerful, artless, and wholly denotative visual empiricism, these early instrumental uses of photographic realism were systematized on the basis of an acute recognition of the inadequacies and limitations of ordinary visual empiricism. Thus two systems of description of the criminal body were deployed in the 1880s; both sought to ground photographic evidence in more abstract statistical methods.[36]

Bertillon's cards represent one of these descriptive systems, becoming the most common and useful practice of criminal identification in the twentieth century, a practice adopted by police departments on both sides of the Atlantic. Yet the combined images and physical descriptions on the backs of *Albert Johnson* and *Edward Cooper* are not proof of anything, except perhaps that these two young men existed and were apprehended by the New York City police in 1908. It was the organization of cards such as these into a comprehensive and accessible filing system—creating an extensive and functional criminal archive—that was Bertillon's real contribution to police work and the growth of social regulation. Hence we stumble upon another of photography's main functions, that of the *archive.*

In both the public and private spheres, photographs preserve, systematize, and save visual information. The Bertillon Card, or mug shot, described above is just one example of photography's archival function. Photographs produced for medical, scientific, and industrial purposes similarly fulfill archival needs and photographs have long been used in the formation of personal and familial archives, with the family album as the most prevalent example. Throughout the nineteenth and twentieth centuries photography was the primary means for the creation and expression of personal and familial identities, and photography, either analog or digital, continues to serve the individual and the family today.

Nineteen Photo Booth Portraits (c. 1940) [page 41] illustrates a collection of friends and perhaps loved ones, organized around the larger portrait of a young woman at the center of the album page. The photographs create a fascinating visual and conceptual grid of smiling and animated faces posing for the photo booth portrait. Each image is unique, like the personalities represented, yet the stories of these individuals and the woman in their midst—the details of their relationships, connections, hopes, dreams, and lives—are lost to us. We are left to wonder: who were these people, how were they connected, and who assembled them here on this album page?

Scholars have identified a variety of social roles performed by album keepers. In her study of photographic albums, Martha Langford has emphasized that album producers are themselves part of the social dynamics mapped on the pages of a photo book, and arranged photographs so as to articulate their own internal experience of the family; thus she noted "the family compiler may be the daughter to one woman and the sister to another; she lives, and not solely through the lives of others; her voice could never be objective or omniscient, however neutral or complete her album's overall effect."[37] Speaking of a specifically female album maker, Langford suggests the ways that the compiler—often one person per family—created her own reading of the family dynamic.

Cousin Phill's Page, Sept. 29, 38 [page 47], another loose album page, reveals the hand of the album compiler through the handwritten inscriptions accompanying the photographs, the title caption at top, and the inclusion of the date "Sept.

29, 38" at the bottom. Clearly Phil, pictured at center, is the subject, but not the maker, of the album, a point underscored by the misspelling of his name in the title caption. He is depicted in a United States Navy flyer's outfit, standing alongside a Grumman scout plane, perhaps the same plane pictured in flight in the top left corner of the page. Together the images document a flyover of the San Francisco Bay area, compiling the interesting sites of the harbor, including Treasure Island, the Golden Gate Bridge, and Alcatraz Island. The specificity of the date implies that this collection records a particular, and likely important, day in Phil's life. Perhaps this was the first time he piloted the plane or the first time he took aerial photographs as a co-pilot? The photographs could be precious documents of the event or they could be the event itself. This may have been a training flight, where both pilot and co-pilot practiced their flying and scouting skills, with the photographs as the desired result. Whatever the exact occasion, *Cousin Phill's Page* assembles an archive of experience that combines elements of private and public meaning, visualizing the unique and irrecoverable experience of the Navy pilot during the interwar years and the common sites of fascination and entertainment that joined San Franciscans of the 1930s and beyond.

Even without the contextual frame of the album, individual family photographs often track people, relationships, and experiences for archival posterity. Although unique to each family, collectively these snapshots tend to fall into predictable and common categories. As an important innovation, George Eastman's Kodak camera triggered the proliferation of the familiar family photograph—the snapshot—by putting photographic technology in the hands of average consumers. Even as technology has changed since the Kodak's inception in the late nineteenth century, the typical iconography of the snapshot has not, as Karl Steinorth outlines in his history of Kodak: "in spite of technical advances, today's snapshooters are generally interested in the very same subjects that interested their predecessors of a hundred years ago. Thus snapshots show a continuing repetition of ever recurring subjects within which, however, a remarkable variety is possible."[38]

Couple Ice Skating (c. 1890) [page 45] and *Boy with Dog* (1891) [page 49] are two lighthearted snapshots that reproduce familiar photographic themes. Representing an interesting spin on the outdoor-themed family image, *Couple Ice Skating* shows a man and a woman, hands locked, taking a twirl on an iced-over lake. These two are the only people visible skating in this cold-weather vista. Who is the third person in their party with camera in hand: a friend, a family member, or possibly a child? Was the goal to document a beginning skater or an expert? Was this the first safe skating day of the season or the last? Or is the photograph a remnant of a purely spontaneous occurrence? Unmarked by inscriptions, and long removed from its original familial context, *Couple Ice Skating* suggests some of the difficulties facing the vernacular historian attempting to reconstruct the everyday archives of family imagery.

Boy with Dog, meanwhile, is a charming example of the classic child-and-pet photograph, which offers more access (however indirect) to the family relations framing its content. Here the boy crouches next to the small dog, pictured at the very foreground of an expansive lawn. Seen in the distance, just behind the boy's right ear, is a man standing on the porch. If this is the boy's father, who is the photographer: the boy's mother, a sibling, another family member, or a neighbor? Though these questions are difficult to resolve, snapshots such as *Boy with Dog* nevertheless offer some trace of the intricacies of the family dynamic, detailing the significance of subjects included in, as well as those excluded from, the frame of the lens.

In addition to their private uses, photographs have long served public purposes, recording events for use in public archives: in record keeping, business transactions, and legal proceedings, as well as for identification purposes. A contact sheet for a series of 1921 student portraits from the First Grade at the Bruce School in Lynn, Massachusetts [page 84], functions as both a public and private record. School administrators use such portraits to identify and catalog individual students, and to track class demographics over time. For parents, the class portrait serves as a precious document marking their children's admission into the school system, and thus their participation in civic bureaucracy; it also helps calibrate the child's growth and physical change over time. Families collect, save, and circulate class portraits, proudly sharing the latest images of their children with relatives, friends, and distant loved ones. In these circuits of familial and friendly exchange, the photograph quantifies the health, endurance, and success of the family unit, registering the accomplishments and maturation of its members. In their uses by both the school and the family, class portraits provide important archival information, even as they function as a *yardstick*, a standard of measure or judgment.

The delightful portrait from the Bruce School depicts an intriguing and dynamic group of young students. Each child sits, perhaps at a desk, with arms crossed, resting on the desktop. Although collectively they enact a similar pose, the variety of character is striking: there is little similarity from image to image, and certainly no monotony. Each child expresses a distinctive personality. They all pose, and sometimes even perform, for the camera. Some children smile politely, some grin or even grimace. Their faces are joyful, frightened, complaisant, or bewildered. Some appear more playful: the boy in the third row down, third from the left, toys with the camera, twisting his body and inserting his left shoulder into the scene, so as to display the insignia on his sleeve. The girl pictured above him, eyes bright and clear, smiles matter-of-factly for the camera. And the boy at the top row center cocks his head back slightly, clearly less than comfortable in front of the camera.

One element that sets the vernacular photograph apart from many artistic forms of photography is the importance of seemingly accidental or subsidiary elements to the meaning of the photographic object, including the reverse, matt, frame, casing, presentation, notations, and so forth. Such important yet secondary details are sometimes overlooked in pho-

tographic histories that concentrate on the purely aesthetic image. These aspects of the photograph, and the patterns of handling they often reveal—evidence of wear, use, and possible misuse of the photographic object—hold clues to purpose and meaning. When we turn *1st Grade Bruce School, W. Lynn, Mass, Nov. 1921* over, we discover that someone has carefully stenciled a grid on the back, and inside each meticulously drawn square is the first and last name of the student depicted on the front. This specific information turns the photograph into a more substantial record. Did this photographic sheet belong to the teacher of the class? Did administrators use it to identify and remember the students? Was it part of the school's records? Or did it belong to the family of one of the students depicted? Answers to these questions elude us. The photograph provides a wealth of data, but many of the links required to decipher it are already severed.

In contrast, photography's effectiveness as an empirical tool for use in science and medicine is indisputable. The *Photographische Sternkarten, March 6, 1902* [page 75] and *X-ray of a Human Hand* (c. 1900) [page 76] are two examples of photographs used to study and evaluate visual phenomena not available to the human eye. The *Photographische Sternkarten* (Photographic Star Chart), published in the early twentieth century by Austrian astronomer Johann Palisa and German astronomer Max Wolf, represents one page of the first photographic star atlas. Wolf pioneered the use of astrophotography to detect asteroids, and together with Palisa they produced 210 Palisa-Wolf start charts. *X-ray of a Human Hand*, on the other hand, is an early experiment with X-ray technology. Radiography was discovered in 1895 by German professor William Roentgen, who noted that the use of an electrostatic charge passing through a tube created a fluorescent effect. He called these new rays "X-rays," and created the first stable image using his wife's hand as the model. With the gradual dissemination and popularization of Roentgen's process, novelty X-ray images became widely attainable and were sold at fairs and expositions. Produced by the Drake Brothers Studio, this early radiograph of a hand, which repeats Roentgen's first experiments, is likely an early novelty object of this type.

Photographic novelties and collectibles come in a variety of genres, with images of celebrities and erotic pin-ups as the most common examples. *Golden Dreams* combines both of these genres, depicting the young Marilyn Monroe in the nude, prior to her rise to stardom [page 81]. Now infamous and iconic, the "Red Velvet" image appeared as the centerfold in the first issue of *Playboy* magazine in 1953, and set the visual terms for the magazine's subsequent photographic layouts. As a functioning calendar, however, the photo-object included in the exhibition projected the eroticized icon beyond the private experience of the magazine centerfold. Combining social utility and erotic titillation, the calendar provided viewers in auto repair garages, machine shops, warehouses, barrooms, and other spaces of working-class labor and leisure with standardized fantasies intended to mitigate the passing of time, ease the experience of physical work, and focus and delimit the desires explored in free time. The photograph also operates as a benchmark for female erotic perfection, reaffirming Marilyn Monroe's image as a standard for female beauty. However unrealistic or unattainable to most women, Monroe's figure was nevertheless continually promoted as the epitome of classic American beauty in twentieth-century popular culture.

Another form of standardized erotic culture appears in *Nature Beauty*, a lenticular postcard of a nude woman dating from the 1970s [page 66]. Lenticular images, like stereographs [pages 64–65], create an impression of three-dimensionality in a two-dimensional image. The process involves several photographs of an object interlaced and combined with a lenticular lens to generate one image with depth. A format for popular collectibles, the lenticular postcard is often laminated, creating a high-gloss end result. *Nature Beauty* was likely this kind of collectible and represents an enigmatic, yet available, image of a nude young woman. Set in "nature," a background forest of trees, the woman offers herself to the viewer, hands raised above her head and grasping a tree trunk. The 3-D effect further enhances the thrill of this offering. The goal of the photo-object is to lure the viewer into the scene, creating the illusion that he is actually standing right next to the tempting young woman: you could just reach out and touch her. In this way, *Nature Beauty* demonstrates a sense of photographic immediacy and illustrates its function as *surrogate*: as a substitute or stand-in for experience.

Travel photographs, including the four stereo cards from the Frank M. Good Studio in London [pages 64–65], are another photographic genre designed to create the illusion of "being there." Novelty and keepsake images have taken this idea further, allowing the traveler to bring the trip home in the form of photographic souvenirs. *Grand Junction, Colorado* (c. 1930) [page 67], a cyanotype photograph on a fabric bandana, depicts nine views of Grand Junction, a popular tourist site. Likely a travel souvenir, the bandana could have been obtained as a memento, or as a gift for someone who was unable to make the trip. As a representation of the place, the keepsake helps to remember, or simulates, the experience of being there.

Man with Carnival Cutout (c. 1900) [page 66] offers another kind of photographic souvenir. The tintype pictures a man posing in a comical cutout scene of a couple in a tilting rowboat about to capsize. The woman's cartoonish face exhibits a ghastly expression that contrasts starkly, and humorously, with the calm smirk on the face of the sitter poking his head through the cutout. The artificiality of the sitter's implication in the melodramatic scene is underscored by the carnival photographer's lackadaisical cropping: if you look very closely at the bottom of the image, you can see the man's trousers just under the bottom of the frame of the cutout. The cardboard cutout obviously rests in the man's lap, a detail that whimsically undermines the illusion of the painted scene. Cutouts of this kind were popular novelty attractions at carnivals, circuses, and other sites of public entertainment throughout the twentieth century (they still exist today, though largely in digital format). In all these iterations, the carnival cutout remade the creation of a portrait photograph as a humorous event in itself, an experience of playful performance. The photographs that result from these performances register a moment of carnivalesque entertainment, in which the sitter tries on a different persona in a surreal situation, for the amusement of family members, friends, or loved ones. As such, images like *Man with Carnival Cutout* offered their owners souvenirs of the shared, and otherwise irrecoverable, experience of playful transgression at the fair; in writing on the souvenir, Susan Stewart reminds us:

> We might say that this capacity of objects to serve as traces of authentic experience is, in fact, exemplified by the souvenir. The souvenir distinguishes experiences. We do not need or desire souvenirs of events that are repeatable. Rather we need and desire souvenirs of events that are reportable, events whose materiality has escaped us, events that thereby exist only through the invention of narrative.[39]

As a pictorial record of a moment of comical performance that only took shape in the photographer's tent, *Man with Carnival Cutout* offers its viewer a material stand-in for an event "whose materiality has escaped us," a surrogate for a bit of play-acting with painted representation that was unrepeatable outside of the carnival.

Whether stashed in a wallet or purse, worn as a badge or pin, concealed in a locket or watch, or downloaded and exchanged on cellular phones and other electronic devices, photographs have long been carried on the person as reminders of loved ones or substitutes for absent associations. *World War II Soldier's Pocket Album* (c. 1943) [page 73] is a small folio designed specifically for a soldier to hold and handle during the war. This album includes several small black-and-white images of soldiers, family, and friends, neatly housed and folded in the green leather album. The soldier could keep it safe in his pocket and consult its contents during times of stress, trauma, or fear, as a means of comfort while long separated from the solace of the domestic sphere.

Carefully containing and preserving a series of family images against the ravages of time, violence, and uncertainty, *World War II Soldier's Pocket Album* suggests the importance of durability and material longevity to the function of the photographic surrogate. The private and portable album, moreover, suggests a wider range of vernacular photographic objects that have been carefully produced and conscientiously maintained by everyday people, objects that include *fotoescultura* (photosculptures made in Mexico), scrapbooks, and travelogues.[40] As photographic technology has modernized, however, vernacular practices involving craftsmanship and preservation have yielded to a body of everyday photographic forms organized around speed and disposability.

The desire for immediate photographic representations—now sated with digital images—initially led to the instant imaging technology best popularized by Polaroid in the 1970s. The anonymous *Bullfight* is a relatively early Polaroid SX-70 photograph, the format that came to most signify Polaroid during the last decades of the twentieth century [page 73]. The excitement of Polaroid technology rested not only in the immediate gratification of the instant image—offering the ability to experience an event firsthand and as photographic spectacle at nearly the same time—but also in the possibility of quickly sharing and circulating the hand-held image. The Polaroid process capitalized on the pleasure of the photographic moment, reiterating that moment as a spontaneous, and often collective, event. Although far removed from the action in the bullring, *Bullfight* maintains the traces of immediacy and action that inspired its initial production, capturing the charging bull and its human challenger moments before their (potentially) deadly confrontation. In its narrative irresolution (the "victory" is forever deferred), the instant image offered its viewer an effective surrogate for the tension at the center of the spectatorial experience of the bullfight.

Bullfight is the only truly "found" photograph in the Kingston Collection, having been noticed on the street and picked up by the collector. Quickly made, enjoyed for a time, and discarded, the instant image represents a new mass of photographic practices defined by instantaneous production and rapid obsolescence. And yet, as an everyday object made for a specific purpose that subsequently found its way into the hands of a collector far removed from its original, contextual function, *Bullfight* invokes the trajectories traced by all the images in the exhibition, however rapidly or deliberately produced and consumed. As an image discarded and "rediscovered," the Polaroid challenges us to consider the character of photographic overproduction and the motives guiding the scholarly recuperation of super-abundant everyday photographs. A symbol of the immeasurable photographic surplus in the world, this one image reminds us of just how much photographic junk is still out there, everywhere, and suggests that the conditions of overabundance have long defined the production and consumption of everyday photography.

Indeed, there is an unknown surfeit of nineteenth- and twentieth-century photographic images available for distribution and consumption. Given this plentiful body of material, it is perhaps surprising that the collectible market in vernacular photography is booming. The sheer scope and ordinary character of works ready for collecting would seem to complicate the organization of a vernacular photography market around traditional value determinants (rarity, preciousness of materials, etc.). Nevertheless, dealers and collectors are acquiring vernacular photographs with a growing intensity. This market boom seems to reflect cultural preoccupations outside of customary market maneuvering. Thus Geoffrey Batchen has argued that the market in old photographs is stimulated by a sense of nostalgia:

> For us today, these nineteenth-century images might even evoke another kind of memory—nostalgia. Involving an illogically warm feeling toward the past, a kind of pleasurable sadness, nostalgia was regarded as a neurosis in previous centuries and thought to be manifest by a swelling of the brain. Now, of course, the stimulation of nostalgia is a major industry—the past has become a profitable commodity.[41]

For Batchen, then, the accelerating vernacular photography market can be understood as a manifestation of a broader trend toward the commodification of nostalgia, a trend manifested elsewhere in amusement parks, historical museums, and history-themed television programming. The nostalgia provoked by vernacular photographs might be understood as two-pronged: a reflection of our desire to hold on to the twentieth century on the one hand, and, on the other, a longing for the lost paper print and celluloid negative, as the analog image is replaced by the digital.

In organizing our exhibition of vernacular photography, we have participated in, and contributed to, this burgeoning interest in the everyday image. In so doing, however, we have proposed a historiographic framework that challenges the perceived separation of past and present driving nostalgic reappropriations of vernacular photography, a framework that instead stresses the bonds joining contemporary and historical photographic practices. As much as the means of obtaining a photographic image have changed in past decades, the uses of these images, as characterized in this essay, still persist. Photography still defines the overwhelmingly image-suffused experience of contemporary life, and photographs continue to satisfy a variety of social needs. In emphasizing broad and overlapping categories of social use (Proof, Archive, Yardstick, Surrogate), we have hoped to suggest the outlines of an historical approach that can account for both the dynamic social functions that photography has played in the everyday life of today and the distant past, and the growing centrality of photographic practice to modern social existence. That approach, however, must also account for the processes by which everyday people learned to understand, use, reshape, and contest photographs and photographic practices. Discussing the importance of the daguerreotype—the first popular photographic medium—as a social and cultural phenomenon in the nineteenth century, Merry Foresta writes, "to discover yourself already positioned in time and space, to pose, to regard what you see as the product of a viewpoint, to travel backward from appearances to the eye: these exercises are part of a contemporary way of life. Today the marvel of photography—seen everywhere, used by everyone—is easy to forget."[42] Vernacular photography, as a field of study, must consider the expansiveness of photographic practice and its continuing status as a "marvel," an object of wonder, surprise, and even anxiety. By studying vernacular photographic objects closely for traces of the hopes, desires, anxieties, and frustrations that everyday people have brought to bear on photographs and photographic activities, and connecting these traces across temporal, geographical, and media borders, we can begin to account both for the "marvel" of photography and its ever-expanding ubiquity.

1. Geoffrey Batchen, "Vernacular Photographies," *History of Photography* 24, no. 3 (Autumn 2000): 262.

2. Kouwenhoven first presented "Living in a Snapshot World" as a lecture sponsored by the Museum of Modern Art and the Metropolitan Museum in New York in 1972. Portions of the essay were published in *Aperture* in 1974, and later in his 1982 collection of essays, *Half a Truth is Better Than None*. See John A. Kouwenhoven, "Living in a Snapshot World" and "Photographs as Historical Documents," in *Half a Truth is Better Than None: Some Unsystematic Conjectures about Art, Disorder, and American Experience* (Chicago: University of Chicago Press, 1982).

In these essays, Kouwenhoven also outlined a notion of the "democratization of vision" engendered by photography. Citing Kouwenhoven as an inspirational source, Rodger Kingston also provides his critique of the omission of the vernacular from traditional histories of photography. Kingston offers an "alternative history of photography" in his self-published essay, "An Alternative History of Photography" (1982). Kingston continued to develop these ideas in subsequent essays and talks, including his lecture at the Boston University Art Gallery's 2004 conference, *Vernacular Reframed*. On Kingston and his collection, see Rosalind Smith, "Rodger Kingston's Forgotten Photographs: A Collector of the Not-So-Famous Image Makers," *Shutterbug* 26, no. 10 (August 1997): 74–75, 80; and Daile Kaplan's essay, "Photography's New Identity & The Kingston Collection," in this volume.

3. A. D. Coleman, "Quotidian or vernacular photography: Premises, functions and contexts," *Impact of Science on Society* 42, no. 4 (1992): 315.

4. Ibid., 316.

5. Dave Kenyon, *Inside Amateur Photography* (London: B. T. Batsford Ltd., 1992), 10 and 25.

6. Elizabeth Hutchinson quoted in "Vernacular Photographies: Responses to a Questionnaire," *History of Photography* 24, no. 3 (Autumn 2000): 229–230.

For a more thorough introduction to the use of the "vernacular" terminology, particularly as it evolved out of vernacular architecture studies, see Bernard L. Herman's essay, "Vernacular Trouble: Exclusive Practices on the Margins of an Inclusive Art," in this volume.

7. See, for example, Dell Upton and John Michael Vlach, *Common Places: Readings in American Vernacular Architecture* (Athens: University of Georgia Press, 1985); Thomas Carter and Bernard L. Herman, eds., *Perspectives in Vernacular Architecture* (Columbia, MO: University of Missouri Press, 1989); and Jules Prown, "The Truth of Material Culture: History or Fiction?" in *American Artifacts: Essays in Material Culture* (East Lansing, MI: Michigan State University Press, 2000).

8. Pierre Bourdieu, *Photography: A Middlebrow Art* (Stanford, CA: Stanford University Press, 1990); Susan Sontag, *On Photography* (New York: Farrar, Straus and Giroux, 1973); and Roland Barthes, *Camera Lucida: Reflections on Photography* (New York: Farrar, Straus and Giroux, Hill and Wang, 1981).

Other original sources that have contributed to the field of vernacular photography include: John Tagg, *The Burden of Representation: Essays on Photographies and Histories* (Minneapolis: University of Minnesota Press, 1988); and Alan Trachtenberg, *Reading American Photographs: Images as History, Mathew Brady to Walker Evans* (New York: Hill and Wang, 1989).

9. For a review of the Phillips exhibition, see David Wright, "Photography: Questions about the Vernacular," *The New Criterion* 8 (October 1989): 46–50. Other noteworthy exhibitions with publications include: John B. Cameron and William B. Becker, *Photography's Beginnings: A Visual History: Featuring the Collection of Wm. B. Becker* (Rochester, MI: Oakland University, Meadow Brook Art Gallery, 1989); and L. A. Koltun and A. J. Birrell, *Private Realms of Light: Amateur Photography in Canada, 1839–1940* (Markham, Ontario: Fitzhenry & Whiteside, 1984).

10. Geoffrey Batchen, *Photography's Objects* (Albuquerque, NM: University of New Mexico Art Museum, 1997). Batchen's exhibition was on view from August 26 to October 31, 1997. Douglas R. Nickel, *Snapshots: The Photography of Everyday Life, 1888 to the Present* (San Francisco: San Francisco Museum of Modern Art, 1998). Nickel's exhibition was on view from May 22 to September 8, 1998.

11. See Mia Fineman, *Other Pictures: Anonymous Photographs from the Thomas Walter Collection* (Albuquerque, NM: Twin Palms Publishers, 2000); Stephen White and Andreas Blühm, *The Photograph and the American Dream 1840–1940* (Amsterdam: Van Gogh Museum, distributed in the United States by Distributed Art Publishers, New York, 2001); Daile Kaplan, *Pop Photographica: Photography's Objects in*

Everyday Life, 1842–1969 (Toronto: Art Gallery of Ontario, 2003); Brian Wallis and Deborah Willis, *African American Vernacular Photography: Selections from the Daniel Cowin Collection* (New York: International Center of Photography, 2005); and Sarah Greenough, Dianna Waggoner, Sarah Kennel, and Matthew S. Witkovsky, *The Art of the American Snapshot, 1888–1978* (Princeton, NJ: Princeton University Press, 2007). This is only a partial list. See the bibliography in this volume for a more comprehensive list of exhibitions.

12. See John Ibson, *Picturing Men: A Century of Male Relationships in Everyday American Photography* (Washington, DC: Smithsonian Institution Press, 2002); Mark Michaelson and Steven Kasher, *Least Wanted: A Century of American Mugshots* (New York and Göttingen, Germany: Steven Kasher Gallery and Steidl, 2006); and Robert Bogdan and Todd Weseloh, *Real Photo Postcard Guide: The People's Photography* (Syracuse, NY: Syracuse University Press, 2006). The bibliography in this volume lists many more examples.

13. Batchen, "Vernacular Photographies," 268 and 263.

14. A 2002 special edition of *Afterimage* devoted to vernacular photography followed this important issue. See *Afterimage* 29, no. 6 (May-June 2002).

15. Douglas R. Nickel, quoted in "Vernacular Photographies: Responses to a Questionnaire," 229. Nickel offers a thorough and brilliantly articulated overview of the development of the history of photography as a field of study, as well as its inherent limitations, in "History of Photography: The State of the Research," *The Art Bulletin* 83, no. 3 (September 2001): 548–558.

16. Hunt, quoted in "Vernacular Photographies: Responses to a Questionnaire," 230–231.

17. Edwards, quoted in "Vernacular Photographies: Responses to a Questionnaire," 231.

18. Hutchinson, quoted in "Vernacular Photographies: Responses to a Questionnaire," 230.

19. Edwards, quoted in "Vernacular Photographies: Responses to a Questionnaire," 230.

John Ibson has pointed to these two distinct approaches to vernacular photography, arguing that scholars, when confronted with an "old" photograph have tended to achieve either a "better understanding of the cultural moment when the picture was taken" or "use the image as a vehicle not so much to the past as to the present day" (Ibson, *Picturing Men*, 198). For an insightful overview of the relationship between vernacular photography and cultural studies, see Ibson's "Epilogue: Out of the Attic—Vernacular Photography and Cultural Studies," in *Picturing Men*, 197–201.

20. Batchen, "Vernacular Photographies," 263.

21. Batchen, *Forget Me Not: Photography and Remembrance* (New York: Princeton Architectural Press, 2004), 15.

22. Elizabeth Edwards and Janice Hart, eds., *Photographs Objects Histories: On the Materiality of Images* (London: Routledge, 2004).

23. Douglas R. Nickel, "The Snapshot—Some Notes," in *Snapshots: The Photography of Everyday Life, 1888 to the Present*, 13.

24. Ibid.

25. Ibid., 14.

26. Ibid., 13.

27. Ibid.

28. See Greenough et al., *The Art of the American Snapshot, 1888–1978*, and Barbara Levine and Stephanie Snyder, *Snapshot Chronicles: Inventing the American Photo Album* (New York: Princeton Architectural Press, 2006). Several typos in the text of *Snapshot Chronicles* indicate that it was not carefully edited from a scholarly perspective.

29. On the framing of the exhibition, see http://www.nga.gov/exhibitions/snapshotinfo.shtm, as well as Sarah Greenough's introduction to the exhibition catalogue in Greenough et al., *The Art of the American Snapshot, 1888–1978*. Although we question the aesthetic premise of the exhibition, the importance of the substantial catalogue essays by Waggoner, Kennel, Greenough, and Witkovsky, as well as the technical timeline included in the catalogue, are not to be overlooked.

For a classic aestheticizing treatment of vernacular images, see John Szarkowski, *The Photographer's Eye* (New York: Museum of Modern Art, 1966). And on the "snapshot aesthetic" popular in art photography practice during the 1970s, see Jonathan Green, *The Snap-Shot* (Millerton, NY: Aperture, 1974). Geoffrey Batchen offers his reading of the snapshot "as a complex social device rather than simply as a static art object" and also provides an incisive critique of recent exhibitions that isolate snapshots from any original context in his essay, "From Infinity to Zero," in *Now Is Then: Snapshots from the Maresca Collection*, by Marvin Heiferman, Geoffrey Batchen, and Nancy Martha West (New York: Princeton Architectural Press, 2008).

30. For a recent historical treatment of the photographic album, see Elizabeth Siegel, "'Miss Domestic' and 'Miss Enterprise': *Or, How to Keep a Photograph Album*," in *The Scrapbook in American Life*, edited by Susan Tucker, Katherine Ott, and Patricia P. Buckler (Philadelphia: Temple University Press, 2006).

31. Brian Wallis, "The Dream Life of a People: African American Vernacular Photography," in *African American Vernacular Photography*, 9–10.

32. Batchen, "Vernacular Photographies," 263.

33. Roland Barthes, *Camera Lucida*, 88–89, 76.

34. Susan Stewart, *On Longing: Narratives of the Miniature, the Gigantic, the Souvenir, the Collection* (Durham: Duke University Press, 1993), 122–123. Stewart's analysis here refers specifically to Tom Thumb, or miniature wedding events in the 1950s; her argument

regarding the photographic spectacle of the modern wedding, however, has broad social and cultural implications.

35. "Augutus Roycroft Draft Registration Card," Granville County, North Carolina, Roll 1765645, *World War I Draft Registration Cards, 1917–1918*, http://search.ancestrylibrary.com (accessed February 10, 2008), and "Augustus Roycroft," Dutchville, Granville, North Carolina, Enumeration District 79, Image 730, *U.S. Federal Census 1910* (Provo, UT: The Generations Network, 2006), http://search.ancestrylibrary.com (accessed February 10, 2008).

36 Allan Sekula, "The Body and the Archive," *October* 39 (Winter, 1986): 18. In addition to a comparison of the identification methods and goals of Bertillon and Francis Galton, Sekula offers a thorough argument regarding the model of the archive as a key to photographic meaning in the nineteenth century and its importance to the establishment of modern regulatory bureaucracies. On photography as an instrument of power, see also John Tagg, *The Burden of Representation*. On crime and photography, see Sandra Phillips, *Police Pictures: The Photograph as Evidence* (San Francisco: Chronicle Books, 1997), and Mark Michaelson and Steven Kasher, *Least Wanted.*

37. Martha Langford, *Suspended Conversations: The Afterlife of Memory in Photographic Albums* (Montreal: McGill-Queen's University Press, 2001), 95.

38. Karl Steinorth, "Photography for Everyone," in Steinorth and Colin Ford, eds., *You Press the Button, We Do the Rest* (London: Dirk Nishen Publishing, 1988), 13.

39. Susan Stewart, *On Longing*, 135.

40. On *fotoescultura* see Monica Garza, "Secular *Santos*," in *Afterimage* 29, no. 6 (May-June 2002): 8–9.

41. Batchen, *Forget Me Not*, 14.

42. Merry Foresta, "Secrets of the Dark Chamber: The Art of the American Daguerreotype," in Foresta and John Wood, *Secrets of the Dark Chamber: The Art of the American Daguerreotype* (Washington, DC: National Museum of American Art, Smithsonian Institution Press, 1995), 27.

VERNACULAR TROUBLE:

EXCLUSIVE PRACTICES ON THE MARGINS OF AN INCLUSIVE ART

Bernard L. Herman

Photographs from the Rodger Kingston Collection entice, provoke, and cajole the viewer's imagination into meditations on the objects of photography. The Oliver Dutton household (fieldhands and packers included) [page 78] arrayed in the farmhouse yard in an arc of pride, celebrate the harvest and prosperity. We gaze back over the distances of drought and plenty, boom years and bust, and grasp an illusory permanence anchored in a mechanically fixed moment. The Dutton photograph—indeed the whole of the Kingston Collection— invites us into a world of images seemingly distinguished by their everydayness, but singled out of millions of contemporary images for their aesthetic, lyrical, and narrative power. The image of the Dutton enterprise shares space with unlikely neighbors *Masked Ballerina* (c. 1880) [page 63], *Liggett's Window Display* (c. 1920) [page 80], *Woman and Inflatable Horse in Pool* (c. 1940) [page 49], and *Gunned Down* (c. 1970) [page 69]. The difficulty at the core of such an assemblage is forming a strategy to bring such diverse images into a shared critical space. The notion of vernacular photography provides that means, but it does so from a position of risk.

Vernacular is one of those words we deploy when placing one body of expressive culture in opposition to (or at least in tension with) the perceived powers of a dominant canon. We evoke the vernacular (like *outsider, self-taught, folk,* and even *everyday*) when and where we find it necessary or convenient to grant some degree of legitimacy to the world of aesthetic production that historically has been relegated to the margins of art. We modify the word *photography,* for example, with *vernacular* to establish a quality of difference, and within that difference construct a separate authority. As a consequence, categorizing terms like *vernacular* or *self-taught* or *grassroots* accomplish paradoxical purposes. They focus attention on what is implicitly understood and accepted as occupying a margin of cultural production. These categories succeed, though, because they are dependent on the tacit acceptance of standards against which they are judged and categorized. Categorical terms become the basis for canonical judgments and consequently achieve the authority of categorizations in their own right. By virtue of the oppositional contexts that generated them, these terms sustain and consolidate the power of the art worlds they are intended to contest. *Vernacular* and its cousins, then, are terms that become ideologically suspect in two key ways. First, they valorize objects and images in ways that keep them on the sidelines of art history. Second, they rely on established critical models that substitute one set of hierarchical judgments for another. What to do?

Images in the Rodger Kingston Collection provisionally map the territory of vernacular photography in a way that gestures toward qualities of authorship, subject, aesthetics, audience, and style situated outside a constructed notion of fine-art photography. In a phrase they define themselves by what they are not. The materiality and visuality of their difference, however, is notoriously elusive, powered it seems not by the images themselves but by the ideologies that receive them. The very breadth and diversity of the Kingston Collection underscores the observation that vernacular photography succeeds as a critical practice rather than as a body of images. How else could we account for the relationships between *Boy with Dog* (1891) [page 49], *X-ray of a Human Hand* (c. 1900) [page 76], and *American Woolen Co. Inc.* (c. 1920) [page 52]?

Geoffrey Batchen recognized vernacular trouble at the very outset, observing: "most histories [of photography] tenaciously focused on the artistic ambitions of the medium, excluding all other genres except as they complement a formalist art-historical narrative." He then turned his attention toward the definition of vernacular photography by juxtaposing it with the canonical. Vernacular photographs were generated in great numbers by the self-taught, the working class, the anonymous, the "commercial profiteer." They were idiosyncratic, marginal, and intractable in their relationship to fine-art photography—in a word they were subversive. "So there is a lacuna in photography's history, an absence," Batchen observed, "and we are talking about the absence not just of vernacular photographies themselves, but of a cogent explanation for that absence."[1]

His last point is key. We can certainly construct and contest categories or genres of vernacular photography around qualities of authorship, process, and appearances, but how do we explain absence? To state the problem from another perspective, why is it that we now need a category for vernacular photography, and how is the recognition of this photography implicated by the inclusive and exclusive practices of canonical thinking? An examination of these problems provides elements of a critical framework to guide us through the issues we confront today in vernacular photography as represented in the Kingston Collection. At the same time, I also want to suggest the ways in which the idea of the vernacular has come of age and where we might go from here.

The rise of the vernacular in material culture, decorative arts, visual culture, and image studies springs from several sources. The development of vernacular architecture as the object of study, and as strategies for thinking about those objects, also illustrates the ideological underpinnings of other categories of the vernacular and a possible course for their critical future. As it emerged in the field of architectural history in the United Kingdom and the United States, the designation *vernacular* provided a handle to latch onto all those many thousands of buildings systematically ignored in the prevailing paradigm of architectural history. The term *vernacular* was intended to enfranchise all those buildings routinely alienated from architectural history—but it did so by creating its own criteria. At the outset vernacular buildings were deemed those that were rural, pre-industrial, everyday, and anonymous. Because they stood beyond the pale of architectural history, their study took the form of a continuing critique on the very subject of the discipline.

At the same time that vernacular buildings were deployed to counter the established subjects of architectural history, they also occasioned new methodologies drawn from archaeology, anthropology, linguistics, sociolinguistics, geography, and other fields. Thus, *vernacular* applied to architecture promoted a critique of not just the kinds of buildings worthy of serious study but also of the very ways in which we might most fruitfully study them.[2]

Accommodating the noncanonical ambitions of vernacular architecture studies within vernacular photography relies on a shift from object-centered to object-driven interpretations. Object-centered approaches focus on the artifact as an end in itself, advancing an understanding of why something looks the way it does. Such studies focus, for example, on the specifics of typology, production, or authorship. They stand as a necessary first step to object-driven studies that take these insights and ask the questions of what and how things mean. Although the two approaches cannot exist independent of each other, their relative emphases suggest something of how the idea of the vernacular has evolved. In object-centered approaches there is an implicit sense that we can discern what might be termed *vernacular qualities*. In vernacular architecture studies these include choice and handling of materials, free interpretations of academic styles, types of buildings—and from these observable characteristics vernacular qualities emerged: naïve, conservative, traditional. Object-driven approaches, however, shift the emphasis from the thing itself to the contexts in which objects work as both things and signs. Returning to the idea of vernacular as the language of everyday use, these approaches stress the communicative, performative, and conversational qualities of objects within the infinite contexts in which they were created and used. In a sense, vernacular architecture relocated its emphasis from the explanation *of* objects to questioning the critical spaces *between* objects. The result is the study of things in order to unravel the complexities of cultural production and reception, processes emblematic of constantly shifting everyday human relationships.[3]

As vernacular architecture studies waxed in influence they also produced their own dilemmas. Rooted in oppositional discourse and claiming an ideological high ground, they constructed their own borders, and so became subject to an internal critique that linked "old" vernacular architecture studies to the very architectural history they sought to correct. In its initial formulation, the object of vernacular architecture was the intellectual enfranchisement of all those architectures ignored, disparaged, and marginalized by prevailing, institution-based practices of architectural history. As with vernacular photography, the first level of critique in vernacular architecture studies addressed the lacuna intrinsic to an established, canonical history of architecture.

The paradox at the heart of vernacular architecture centers on defining both its objects (the buildings) and its subjects (questions engendered by buildings). The first attempts at defining vernacular architecture centered on the enumeration of building types, technologies, and styles excluded by an academic or "bookish" architectural history. Because vernacular architecture cast itself as inclusive, it soon grew overwhelmed by ever more varied architectures, to the point where studies in the United States eventually encompassed the kinds of buildings associated with the "old" architectural history—buildings like eighteenth-century Anglican churches and the dwellings of wealthy urban merchant families. Vernacular architecture simply reached an ideological moment when, hemmed in by its own orthodoxies, it could no longer delimit its objects.

The resolution to this impasse took shape in the assertion that what distinguished vernacular architecture studies from other architectural histories was not the buildings they scrutinized but the kinds of questions they asked and how they asked them. Vernacular architecture now defined itself on the basis of how it examined and interpreted buildings of all sorts. That shift, however, did not manifest itself as a uniform critical approach or a school of thought. If pressed, students of vernacular architecture would likely claim the following. First, the object of study is the whole of architectural expression within an expanding range of contexts. Second, the contexts for vernacular buildings could derive from observable traits, historical circumstance, or theoretical position. Third, whatever its origins, the context for examination was related to practice (in the way in which speech, for example, is related to language). This point is crucial in the sense that it provides the means to address very different sorts of architectures within a shared context that is not necessarily hierarchical in nature.[4]

The analogy between buildings and speech, and architecture and language, remains freighted with the kind of flaws expected when a rhetorical relationship is applied too literally and scrutinized too closely. The part of the equation that works (and has the most relevance to vernacular photography) is the situational dimension of speech. Speech is performative; speech communicates; speech is circumstantial; speech is infinitely variable; speech is strategic. Vernacular architecture and vernacular photography share these qualities. *Vernacular* also implies a sense of the immediate and the everyday, not in the sense of what is common and unremarkable, but of what is sensible in the world of everyday discourse.

Contrasted with formal language, the vernacular comprises the linguistic currency of everyday speech. In the study of material culture the idea of the "everyday" borrows heavily from several critical and theoretical sources. As speech the vernacular is variable and nuanced in the sense that it is situational and coded. Interpretations of objects ranging from traditional quilts to the contemporary outsider arts, for example, draw heavily on a distinction between restricted and elaborated linguistic codes, where the former are constituted by a limited, broadly understood range of terms and the latter by complex terms that are less accessible and geared toward assertions of difference. This distinction originally enabled students of objects to address the ways elites articulated identity and consolidated power—and then to suggest ways power could be contested through objects like dress and behaviors—for instance argot or *charivari*. Current explanatory models addressing the creative and conversational contexts for text and object yield a collection of particularly useful approaches: the poetics of implication, lyric possession, *sensus communis*, and comportment. What unites these approaches is a shared engagement with the object and the creative, communicative, and critical contexts it occupies and defines. In the contexts of vernacular arts they are also linked by a quality of everydayness. The idea of "everyday practice" is central to an understanding of the necessity of vernacular photography. Defined as ways of operating in the world and as the substance of social activity, everyday practices provide a strategy for considering the performative nature of things.[5]

The recognition of the lacuna in the history of photography exposed by Batchen's advocacy for vernacular photographies highlights two additional points in our consideration of vernacular trouble. First, because vernacular photography assails the deficiencies of an established field, its advocates were compelled to define what constituted a universe of these images. The danger is clear. Defined on the margins of an exclusive practice, the inclusivity of vernacular photography maps its own borders—which in turn are necessarily exclusive. This is a dilemma at the core of all the *vernaculars* we advance. Vernacular photography implicitly depends on the need for distinctions that are ultimately exclusive in nature and necessary for rhetorical survival. The continuing debates over outsider or self-taught arts exemplify this problem in two ways: term warfare and the introduction of a canon. The latter point is crystallized in a series of single-page articles that continue to appear in the journal *Raw Vision*.

Originally entitled "Classics of Outsider Art" and then "Outsider Classics," the succession of short essays presents a color reproduction of a work by a selected artist and a brief commentary that includes biographical and contextual information—a kind of art appreciation that celebrates and valorizes both the work and its maker. *Raw Vision*, founded to celebrate the *art brut*, outsider, self-taught, grassroots, and vernacular arts, established itself as a voice for marginalized arts and artists. Articles in the journal, which is heavily supported by advertising, introduce and discuss an extraordinary range of artists. The "Classics of Outsider Art" series, however, has transformed those inclusive ambitions into exclusive outcomes. The net effect of the "Classics of Outsider Art" series has been the construction of a canon populated by artists like Martin Ramírez, Sam Doyle, and William Edmondson. The point here is not whether *Raw Vision* is ideologically suspect, but to recognize a fundamental impulse to categorize, judge, place, and contain these works within hierarchies. The result is a double dilemma. First, although the objects that populate these art worlds may change, the ways we value them do not. Second, these strategies grant a measure of critical authority to a constructed margin, but leave it marginal nonetheless. Vernacular photography courts a comparable risk.[6]

Still, the paradox of the vernacular does not address why we need a category for vernacular photography nor does it explain the significance of the Kingston Collection as an entity for resolving that question. Vernacular photography possesses the quality of metanarrative. Read against the corpus of canonical photography, vernacular photography offers a narrative perspective that comments on the larger history of photography from the inside out. The accidental intervention of a photographer's hand or shadow, an advertising image of a boy and girl pondering the workings of a camera, and an album sheet of photo booth portraits share common ground in the ways they are simultaneously a part of and a commentary on the practice and history of photography. *Page from the Charlie King Album* (c. 1890) [page 43] illustrates the slippery metanarrative quality of vernacular photographs as continuing conversations on everyday practice. The five images mounted on the album page feature various groupings of children around Charlie King. Adult women smilingly look on from the background in the uppermost images. The women are white; the children are almost all black. The apparent informality of the moment and shifting cast of characters suggest that the photographer was laboring to capture the particular photograph at the center of the page. The labeling and King's echoing presence in all five shots indicates that he was the photographic subject that animated the moment.

The commentary on vernacular photography embedded in *Page from the Charlie King Album* is rendered problematic by the fact that the page itself poses another possibility. The central image of seven children with Charlie King at their center is labeled "Kindergartners." Is this the *Charlie King Album* or the keepsake of a now-nameless teacher who recorded her service to the urban poor? What we see in the album page is the process of making not just a particular photograph, but also a particular kind of photograph that draws on the conventions of the group portrait, the souvenir, and a homegrown otherness. *Page from the Charlie King Album* implicates a larger photographic process, exemplified by works like *Class Picture of Ethel M. Colcord* (c. 1890–1891) [page 44], *Two Women in front of Capitol Bldg.* (c. 1890) [page 60], *Hunter with Bear* (c. 1920s) [page 56], *The Tarantella, Naples* (1875) [page 71], and *Your Sisters in Southern Seas Send Greetings* (1902) [page 70].

Vernacular photography provides a vital opportunity to interrogate a larger practice. The absence of vernacular photography from the larger history of photography—the critical space where it should exist—has never been complete. Unsung, these photographs have always been there in their metanarrative capacity, and without them the history of photography as we know it could not exist.

What has happened in the history of photography that we are now compelled to marshal the legions of the vernacular? Three things, I think. First, continuing assaults on canonical art worlds in all of their many political contexts has occasioned the need to articulate alternative critical positions and support them with new and different objects. Second, the anarchy of so many histories is ultimately counterproductive in a critical culture that tends to "flatten" difference. Whether we see vernacular photographs as revolutionaries at the gate or the history of photography magnanimously broadening its compass, the effect is much the same: expansive gestures will always be limited by the constraints of making sense. Third, the enfranchisement of vernacular photography resolves little in ongoing struggles for critical power and position in contemporary art worlds. We will always search for a new absence; we will invariably ask ourselves why it exists; and within that critical space we will inevitably consolidate our own interpretive ambitions and advance our own critical needs. And this paradox is the beauty of vernacular trouble.

1. Geoffrey Batchen, *Each Wild Idea: Writing, Photography, History* (Cambridge: MIT Press, 2001), 57–80.

2. There are multiple overviews of the course of vernacular architecture studies in the United Kingdom; see Christopher Dyer, "History and Vernacular Architecture," Eric Mercer, "The Unfulfilled Wider Implications of Vernacular Architecture Studies," and Matthew Johns, "Vernacular Architecture: The Loss of Innocence," all in *Vernacular Architecture* 28 (1997), 1–19. *Perspectives in Vernacular Architecture* 12 (2007), contains a similar collection of essays reflecting work in the United States. See especially Dell Upton, "The Vernacular Architecture Forum at 25," 11–17 and Anna Andrezejewski, "*Perspectives in Vernacular Architecture*, The VAF and the Study of Ordinary Buildings and Landscapes in North America," 55–63.

3. For an excellent introduction to the visual culture of everyday life, see Marita Sturken and Lisa Cartwright, *Practices of Looking: An Introduction to Visual Culture* (Oxford: Oxford University Press, 2001). See also Judy Attfield, *Wild Things: The Material Culture of Everyday Life* (Berg: Oxford, 2000); Arjun Appadurai, "Introduction: Commodities and the Politics of Value," in *The Social Life of Things: Commodities in Cultural Perspective* (Cambridge: Cambridge University Press, 1986), 3–63; Herman, *The Stolen House* (Charlottesville: University Press of Virginia, 1992), 3–9 and Dell Upton, "Architecture in Everyday Life," *New Literary History* 33, no. 4 (Autumn 2002): 707–23. I am indebted to John Styles for our conversations about the distinctions between material culture studies and design history.

4. Dell Hymes, *Foundations in Sociolinguistics: An Ethnographic Approach* (Philadelphia: University of Pennsylvania Press, 1974), 3–66; Basil Bernstein, *Class, Codes and Control: Theoretical Studies Towards a Sociology of Language* (New York: Schocken, 1971 and 1974), 123–56; Michael Ann Williams and M. Jane Young, "Grammar, Codes, and Performance: Linguistic and Sociolingusitic Models in the Study of Vernacular," in Elizabeth Collins Cromley and Carter L. Hudgins, *Gender, Class, and Shelter: Perspectives in Vernacular Architecture* 5 (Knoxville: University of Tennessee Press, 1995), 40–51.

5. Robert Blair St. George, *Conversing by Signs: Poetics of Implication in Colonial New England Culture* (Chapel Hill: University of North Carolina Press, 1998); David S. Shields, *Civil Tongues and Polite Letters in British America* (Chapel Hill: University of North Carolina Press for the Institute of Early American History and Culture, 1997); Susan Stewart, *On Longing: Narratives of the Miniature, the Gigantic, the Souvenir, the Collection* (Durham: Duke University Press, 1993).

6. "Classics of Outsider Art" is a regular feature in the journal *Raw Vision*.

PHOTOGRAPHY'S NEW
IDENTITY & THE KINGSTON COLLECTION
Daile Kaplan

*I suspect that photography, which is certainly one of the most common or garden pastimes
of all of us, is one of the most difficult things to see.*

SAM WAGSTAFF

Photographer Rodger Kingston's vernacular collection was founded on a bold theoretical premise: select family snapshots, travel photos, advertisements, medical and forensic pictures, female nude studies, and portraits by anonymous or commercial practitioners were to be viewed through the same lens as fine art prints by well-known photographers. Kingston's sensibility was influenced by artists who also identified themselves as collectors, notably Pop artist Andy Warhol, a collector whose insatiable appetite for stuff encompassed everything from funky cookie jars to Art Deco furniture, and vernacular visionary Walker Evans, who was drawn to commercial signage and real photo postcards. In the 1970s, a historical juncture when fine art photography itself was considered a disreputable art form, Kingston's inclusive, indeed voracious, recognition of the intrinsic value of photographic imagery speaks to the extraordinary nature of his endeavor.

Like other pioneers of the period, collecting was (and still is) for Kingston inextricably linked with the art of discovery. Regular visits to flea markets, antique fairs and bookshops, as well as friendly trades, are now supplemented with countless hours logged on to eBay. Kingston began building his collection when the photographic market was in its infancy. Although vintage prints by masters of the medium were readily available for relatively modest sums, Kingston consistently sought less conventional examples of photographic expression. A wedding portrait inscribed with the names of the wedding party [page 60]; a class portrait of the First Grade at Bruce School, in Lynn, Massachusetts [page 84]; or a press print of a draped corpse on a city pavement [page 69]. All were highly desirable and greatly undervalued.

From the outset Kingston recognized that so-called "mistakes" (out-of-focus figures represented in flat space) in the first chocolate-toned Kodak photographic images of 1888–1889 had a fresh immediacy that foreshadowed modernist practices. For Kingston a nineteenth-century American Western landscape by an accomplished unknown maker resulted in the same heart-racing palpitations as a magisterial albumen print by Carleton Watkins. Artfully prescient if visually naïve, unattributed photographs can have the same aesthetic impact as a wonderful iconic art photograph. Kingston enthusiastically referred to these choice works as "forgotten masterpieces." Such images now are recognized as the heart of the vernacular idiom. Intriguing to collectors and scholars alike, vernacular pictures and objects continue to be explored for the unexpected manner in which they reshape the medium's identity.

A discussion relating to Kingston's early collecting impulses would be incomplete without mentioning the influence of Sam Wagstaff, who had been curator of paintings at the Wadsworth Atheneum and Detroit Institute of Art. The aristocratic Wagstaff, a paramour and patron of a young photographer named Robert Mapplethorpe, was an august figure, Lincolnesque in stature, who took the photography world by storm. His reputation for having a sophisticated eye and mighty wit has, sadly, been lost to successive generations of photo-historians, curators, and collectors.

In the halcyon early 1970s (an atmosphere Kingston has compared to the California Gold Rush of 1849), a small coterie of devotees constituted the photographic community. Wagstaff, who clearly enjoyed photography's transgressive role in the art world, emerged as an aficionado of all things photographic. He dared viewers to engage with the pleasure of a photograph—not the name of the photographer—while sagely asserting photography's position as the preeminent art form of the twentieth century. He humorously referred to the medium as the "new Esperanto," alluding to the relationship between the constructed language gaining popularity at the time and photography's potential populist reach. Unlike other serious collectors, most of whom were exclusively buying masterworks by better-known figures, he gloriously made no distinction between snapshots, Xeroxes or photocopies, "found" images, real photo postcards, early nineteenth-century European photography, unidentified American landscapes, commercial or arty nudes, and vintage or modern prints. Each image was examined rigorously and evaluated on its own merit.

Wagstaff was not above tweaking the so-called cognoscenti, who regularly disparaged photography as "too mechanical." He cited works by Tom of Finland, a photographer who specialized in homoerotic male nudes, in the same breath as those by Edward Weston. He influenced numerous curators, collectors, and photographers of this "first wave" (Kingston and myself among them) and is considered one of the most respected, original thinker-collectors of that marvelous era. His seminal exhibition at New York University's Grey Art Gallery, in which he masterfully juxtaposed images by known and unknown photographers, included an anonymous snapshot of a gun-toting Bonnie and Clyde alongside an abstract work by the contemporary artist Gerard Incandela. The catalogue for this show, *A Book of Photographs* (New York, 1978) is a much-sought-after classic of photographic literature to this day. Subsequently, his collection was one of several purchased simultaneously by the J. Paul Getty Museum, in 1984, to inaugurate its photography department.

Kingston and Wagstaff were not alone in identifying new collecting trends. Another collector who had a profound, if disparate, orbit was Fred Spira. The founder of Spiratone—the eponymous mail order house of the 1950s–80s specializing in camera lenses, photo gadgets, and whatnots—he acquired items focusing on technical innovations, rather than an artist's *oeuvre*. His remarkable assemblage included products that were used to view photographs, including an ornately carved mahogany Megalethoscope, measuring four feet long, which permitted magnification of photographic prints created for travel or storytelling effects. Handheld viewing devices with black lacquer inlaid with ivory lay on tabletops. Antique Victorian-era wet-plate cameras and mammoth plate-view cameras stood assembled on their original tripods. Kodak's color-coordinated feminine cameras from the 1920s remained in their original boxes. Custom-made 14K gold Leica cameras from the 1930s and numerous photographic-related kinetic toys (like the Zoetrope) appeared on display in his Queens, New York, home. A little-known but exciting sub-genre in his collection was the detective camera, an apparatus disguised in a variety of everyday objects, including purses, pistols, canes, and cosmetic compacts. In this way he also pursued an alternative, multi-faceted approach to collecting within his scientific, and object-oriented, theme.

Spira's collecting tastes distinguished between American and European photographic manifestations. Colorful viewing devices first appeared in France, England, and Germany, targeted to *haute bourgeoisie* consumers. For most of the Victorian era, photography was considered a luxury pursuit. As it advanced and new techniques and novelties arose, however, it began to appeal to a broader spectrum of the public. Spira also cast his expert eye on photography itself, particularly its uses. For example, Queen Victoria was an early champion of photography as both a practitioner and a collector. Spira acquired a Royal family photograph album containing albumen snapshot-like prints of picnics, family and friends, hunts, and deer heads created and compiled by Her Royal Highness. In addition, he eagerly purchased Harvard Class Albums produced during the Civil War; photographs of criminals inspired by Alphonse Bertillon, who devised the first scientific system of personal identification using body measurements, known as anthropometry; and commercial advertising displays to demonstrate photography's diverse applications. Multi-media visual materials evidencing photography's social applications, such as a honeymoon portrait adorned with sprigs of Alpine Edelweiss surrounding the happy couple, also enlarged traditional notions of photography's identity.

Spira's quiet, Old World charm was the perfect counterpoint to Wagstaff's charismatic, cutting-edge sensibility. To the undiscerning viewer their tastes and interests could not be more different. Yet, like Kingston, they were compatriots, champions of vernacular photography. They addressed the medium's inherent complexity as a fine art and populist medium. Not incidentally, they also challenged the prevailing wisdom, still in place today, that the best way to form a collection is to acquire works by well-known artists. Each was fully conversant with photographic history, generous with information, and delighted to discuss his treasures in detail.

While the art establishment and mainstream America disparaged photography as an illegitimate form of creative expression, these collectors saw a mature field that interfaced with science, technology, art history, and photographic history, in addition to popular and material culture. Urbane iconoclasts, they shaped contemporary notions of photographic discourse. For a young curator like myself, the exposure to each man's personal sensibility was a dazzling coming-of-age experience that raised new questions about the field. If the photographic canon was not composed of bodies of work by well-established artists, how might it be structured? Was it necessary for the history of photography to exist autonomously from the history of art, given that photography's popular appeal and myriad novel applications influenced fine artists? In what ways might vernacular imagery and photographic curiosa be integrated into the medium's multi-dimensional landscape?

*   *   *

Kingston and I first met, in 1988, when I was curating an exhibition commemorating the 150th anniversary of photography entitled "Pop Photographica: Photography's Objects in Everyday Life." His obsession with anonymous photographs was legendary in the field and, since my show focused on photography's social history and applications, colleagues suggested I contact him. In the course of preparing for the show we became long-distance friends and spent hours discussing many issues associated with what today would be described as visual culture. Several examples from his personal collection, as well as his own photographs, appeared in the exposition. Works from Spira's collection also appeared on display. In a leap from convention, unusual artifacts referencing the medium's uses, such as a cyanotype pictorial quilt and photographic jewelry by contemporary photographers, also appeared. Finally, there was a theme I called "Snapshots by Bigshots," featuring celebrities' own photographs of their private lives, such as Spira's Queen Victoria album.

Given the shotgun marriage of high and low culture, the established "masterworks" narrative championed by historian Beaumont Newhall proved too anachronistic and restrictive. Kingston, Spira, and Wagstaff had indelibly altered my photographic consciousness. Prints in the show reflected Kingston's insistence on the democratic nature and formal beauty of anonymous images. Attractive technical viewing devices and cameras from Spira's collection demonstrated how utilitarian items were meant to be decorously integrated in to the home. Other images referenced Wagstaff's unabashed disregard of categories such as "high and low art," his firm belief that photographs deserved to be integrated into the fine art canon as is. An unlikely triumvirate, they inspired me to formalize questions for which I, as a curator, had no answers; they also moved me to become a collector myself, in the hopes of resolving those questions.

Some characterize collecting as an art form, which generally means it is considered a creative pursuit. But, as any collector knows, it is also a soul-searching endeavor that relies equally on intellect, emotion, guts, and instinct. Kingston's unflagging enthusiasm helped me understand the fluid nature of what being a collector means. What I originally construed to be a short-term project not unlike curating became a long-term process, both fun and terrifying, that made an impact on my domestic environment and lifestyle. Kingston, an able tutor, introduced me to the rigors of this avocation. My fifteen-year-long (and still counting) adventure resulted in a genre I named "pop photographica," which I defined as one-of-a-kind, everyday, three-dimensional objects adorned with photographic images.

Although I had experimented with collecting, purchasing the odd postcard, book, album, or snapshot, the first artifact I intentionally acquired for this purpose was a circular hat veil display. A flapper-era beauty wearing a fashionable *chapeau* adorned with feathers is represented on a circular sheet of board; actual black veils cover her face. Since my paternal grandmother had been a hat designer during this same period, the 1920s, I was viscerally drawn to the piece but initially resisted purchasing it. After all, what was it? A photographic glossary revealed no term or definition of this sort of photo novelty, nor would one find an existing genre in which to classify it. Nevertheless I was compelled to buy it.

I lived with this item, came to adore its surreal appearance (the dots of the halftone screen depicting the woman's face mimicked the small, dark clusters of the veil itself), and studied it, utterly enchanted but confused. As a commercial artifact highlighted with a picture by an unknown photographer it superficially referenced popular impulses like consumer culture. Yet, had Man Ray been responsible for the wonder-

ful portrait or, if in a Dadaist gesture, Marcel Duchamp had cleverly superimposed the veil, the display would have immediately been thrown into brilliant high relief as a work of art—which was exactly how I thought of it anyway! What were the implications of this object in relation to photography? I was aware that paper collectibles that were thought to fall outside the parameters of art photography were consigned to a broad catchall category known as photographica, and began to see a (pictorial) pattern. Given the emerging post-modernist discourse, the notion of how commercial or consumer culture was associated with popular culture also begged further study. Soon after, I coined the term "pop photographica" to describe this and other objects containing intimate portraits of largely anonymous subjects affixed to handmade objects whose makers are also unknown.

Cultural historian Lawrence Levine has defined popular culture as "the folklore of industrial society." Photography appeared at the start of the industrial revolution and was arguably one of the most popular inventions of the nineteenth century, quickly capturing *haute* tastes in Europe, Asia, and in the United States. By the 1870s, the exponential proliferation of family portraits on cartes-de-visite, cabinet cards, and assorted paper images became affordable to the general public, dramatically reorienting the popular imagination to one transfixed with pictorial images—a development that continues unabated to this day. Pop photographica, a post-modern art form that initially emerged in the Victorian era, casually mixes media and disciplines to demonstrate how photography was assimilated into popular culture.

The origins of pop photographica may be found in the first photograph, the daguerreotype, a one-of-a-kind, silver-coated copper plate available in sizes ranging from ½ x ¼ inch to 9 x 7 inches, in a vertical or horizontal format. While the daguerreotype was a unique photograph startling in its verisimilitude—which is why it eventually eclipsed the photographic technique invented by William Henry Fox Talbot at about the same time—Talbot's negative-positive system is the basis of photography to this day. Negatives, which he called calotypes, which were made on light-sensitive paper that provided the source material for future photographs or prints, known as Talbotypes or salted paper prints—the latter a purplish-toned, lyrical, soft-focus rendering that bore no resemblance to the realistic detail of the daguerreotype. It was not until the 1860s, with the introduction of the wet-collodion process in which negatives were produced on glass and prints on thin albumen paper, that paper photography assumed the exacting standards and overall clarity of daguerreian images.

Due to its delicate surface, the daguerreotype was housed in a hand-tooled leather, or later thermoplastic, case whose external appearance was similar to a miniature book. When opened, the case fit neatly in the palm of one's hand, resulting in a highly personal viewing experience. Pictures of cherished family members were not set into frames or permanently displayed on a wall. Rather, these cased images were tucked away in drawers or stored on mantels (the cases' exteriors were often highly decorative) to be looked at on special occasions. Hundreds of thousands of daguerreotypes were produced annually from the 1840s to the early 1860s. Most were portraits. The nature of the photographic experience was special. Due to the expense of having one's photograph taken, an individual's visit to the photographer was typically a once-in-a-lifetime occurrence. Expert and itinerant daguerreotypists alike were expected not only to render the subject with all the reverence befitting this important occasion but also somehow to capture his or her inner life or soul. How might such treasured images be utilized and made more accessible?

Both photographers and consumers sought ways to assimilate this new form of representation into daily life. The notion that daguerreotypes (and later photographic techniques) lent themselves to ornamentation was not lost on enterprising photographers. Indeed, the daguerreotype's rich silver patina was particularly well suited to premium goods. Handcrafted items to be enhanced with images were made available to the sitter. A handsome fountain pen with a dagurreian headshot measuring one inch in diameter reflected the special status of a gentleman of leisure. A deluxe walnut sewing kit with fleur-de-lis ornamentation and elaborate interior marquetry houses a daguerreotype of a young woman, with later images of her husband and daughter. Jewelry, however, was the most popular accessory. Broaches, pins, rings, earrings, bracelets, and necklaces were generally purchased at the photographer's studio to be highlighted with a photograph. Occasionally, a particularly rare personal accessory comes to market, such as a mysterious-looking item known as a vinaigrette. The green-glass, anchor-shaped vessel, which is adorned with a tiny ambrotype portrait of a Victorian woman, held smelling salts, an item a lady of leisure (who was undoubtedly clad in an unforgiving, whalebone corset) required in her private apothecary.

Later the ambrotype, an image on glass, was one of many nineteenth-century photographic processes to reflect the medium's continual technical advances. Subsequent innovations in photography resulted in techniques that featured a variety of supports: copper, glass, iron, porcelain, milk glass, silk, linen, cotton, leather, aluminum, wood, celluloid, and paper. These, in turn, facilitated a diverse range of photographic objects—clothing, plates, cups, saucers, mirrors, furniture, souvenirs, screens, boxes, and more. However, the daguerreotype is essential to understanding vernacular praxis. In addition to being unique, it is far more prevalent for daguerreotype portraits to be uncredited than not. As a result, collectors focus on an image's craft, condition, and content. To this day, the photography market rewards great images by the celebrated Boston firm of Southworth & Hawes as eagerly as it does extraordinary portraits or gold-mining scenes by unknown daguerreotypists.

Once the photographic technique known as the tintype was introduced in the 1860s, operators specializing in hard (versus paper) images rarely secured credit for the work they produced. A memory jug (in my collection), dated c. 1885, for example, reflects how photography served the broader interests of vernacular culture. The style of the jug demonstrates a popular folk art form, practiced from the late nineteenth through early twentieth centuries. The bottle, which resembles a whiskey jug, is affixed with a colorful tintype portrait and numerous personal mementos (a key, comb, coins, the letter "G") and shards of crockery. A crude patina of gilt is applied for overall effect. It is rare to find examples employing a photographic image.

A standard-size tintype, measuring 3 x 2 inches, depicts a stogie-chomping male laborer proudly sitting before the cameraman. The identity of the subject is unknown; the jug itself is also bereft of a signature. In the folk art community, where such objects have long been accepted as part of our American cultural heritage, concepts of authorship are almost entirely lacking. In *American Vernacular: New Discoveries in Folk, Self-Taught and Outsider Sculpture* (New York: Abrams, 2002) curator Margit Rowell wrote about the obstacles to connoisseurship in folk and outsider art. "There is no structured discourse or chronological stylistic development . . . no aesthetic value system that would help situate and define" folk objects. Indeed, the certainties associated with an artist's style give way to a focus on materials and technique, which also help date an artifact. In this way, three-dimensional vernacular objects are fostering thought-provoking new approaches to evaluating photographs.

With the growing interest in vernacular imagery, it is fascinating to consider how different the history of photography would be had historians elected to include unique examples of anonymous photographs and pop photographica alongside prints by documentary and fine photographers. Yet, from the beginning, historians were careful to distinguish such practices from high-art endeavors. In *The History of Photography* (New York: The Museum of Modern Art, 1937), the first formalized photographic history text, Beaumont Newhall acknowledged George Eastman's invention of the Kodak camera, citing its "democratization of photography," but did not fully address the important function such pictures provided. Newhall was intent on establishing a pantheon of American photographers, recognizable names whose iconic images would focus attention on masters who employed photography as a medium of self-expression, as did British historians Helmut and Alison Gernsheim, who co-authored a parallel history focusing on European photographers.

There were isolated efforts to redress this situation. Michel Braive's *The Social Photograph* (McGraw-Hill: New York and Toronto, 1966), described what happened to photographs once they were created. This important account emphasized photography's impact on and integration into society. Another, little-known landmark of photographic literature, *Photographic Amusements, Including a Description of a Number of Novel Effects Obtainable with the Camera* (New York: The Photographic Times Publishing Association, 1905), revealed how photography brokered a new visual language at the interstices of the fine and applied arts. Edited by Frank Fraprie and Walter Woodbury, the book was continuously in print from 1896 to 1918, and was revised and republished in the postwar period, remaining in print until 1938—making it one of the most successful photography titles ever published. Chapter headings in early Victorian editions, "Distorted Images" and "Composite Photography," foreshadow techniques adopted by avant-garde artists André Kertész and László Moholy-Nagy in the 1920s. Other chapters, such as "Spirit Photography," "Night Photography," "Luminous Photography," and "Photographs on Apples or Eggs" reveal the odd enthusiasms of professional and hobbyist alike.

Today the classical photography and contemporary art worlds mirror Kingston's vision. Cultural sensitivities to highbrow and lowbrow tastes have collapsed as photography's transparency becomes more evident. Vintage fine-art photographs by blue-chip artists are exhibited in museums around the world and routinely sell for seven figures. Vernacular photography, which has been the subject of several scholarly books and exhibitions, is the darling of the smart set. The ambiguous relationship associated with a sublime amateur snapshot, or a handsome homemade object adorned with an anonymous photographic image, is now accepted as a legitimate expression of the genre. Photography has a new, multi-faceted identity and photographic discourse will never be the same.

ARCHIVE

Archive refers to the ways that photographs are used publicly and privately to organize, preserve, and create memories and social identities. In the private sphere, photographs have long participated in the construction of personal and family histories. The family album is a complex record of familial and friendly relationships, each structured with its own narratives of rivalry, pain, community, and camaraderie.

In the public sphere of modern life, police departments use photographs to preserve instances of crime for posterity. Sociologists and historians use them to complement information-gathering surveys. Medical researchers produce and collect photographs of unusual diseases for future reference. Taken out of their original context as documents, these photographs now serve as fascinating visual histories.

Nineteen Photo Booth Portraits, an album page probably made in the 1940s, sets a constellation of friends, acquaintances, and possibly relatives around the larger, central photograph of the page's presumed owner. Much like twenty-first-century photo-sharing Web sites such as Facebook.com or MySpace.com, this twentieth-century photographic object charts in pictures the friendships and loves of a group of peers at a particular moment in time. Even without the physical template of the album, an individual or family collection of portraits constitutes a storehouse of memory and experience that could be edited and rearranged as the relationships to which they referred flourished or suffered.

Anonymous
Nineteen Photo Booth Portraits, c. 1940
Gelatin silver prints mounted on paper
Approximately 1⅞ x 1½" each with variations; center image 3¼ x 2½"

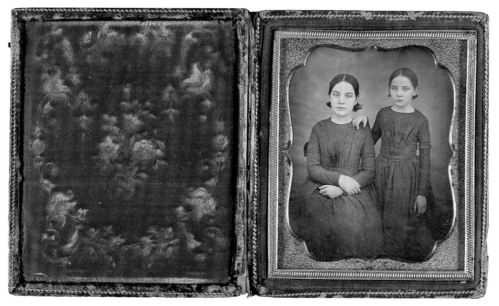

Anonymous
Sisters, c. 1850
Daguerreotype in original case
2¾ x 2¼"

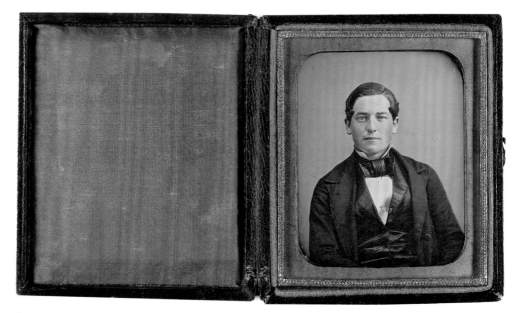

Anonymous
Young Man, c. 1850
Daguerreotype, hand-colored, in original case
2¾ x 2¼"

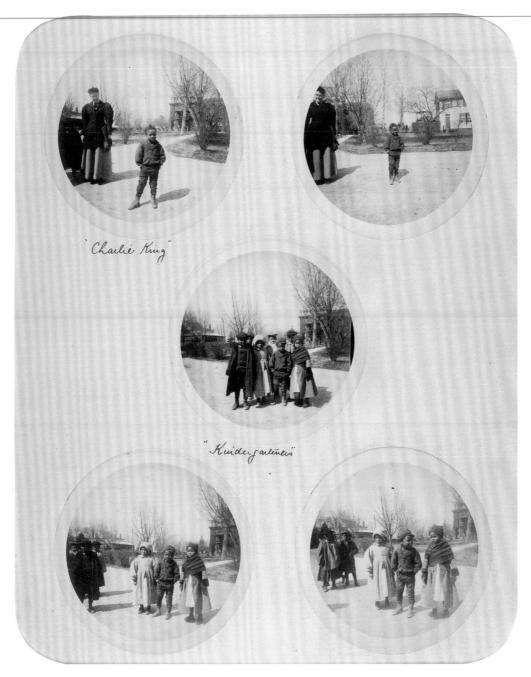

Anonymous
Page from the Charlie King Album, c. 1890
Five Kodak #1 photographs. Albumen prints mounted on cardboard and inscribed
2¼ x 2¼" (each image)

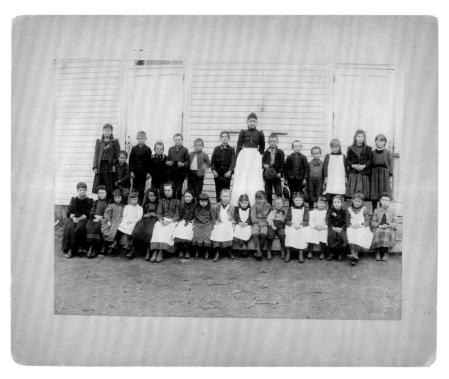

Anonymous
Class Picture of Ethel M. Colcord, c. 1890–1891
(recto & verso)
Albumen print mounted on cardboard,
inscribed on verso
5¾ x 8³⁄₁₆"

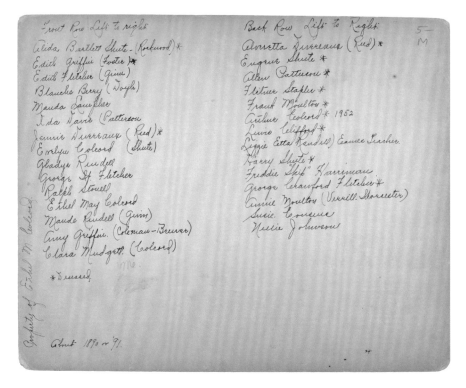

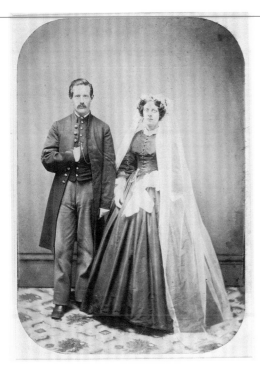

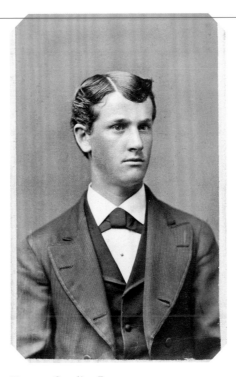

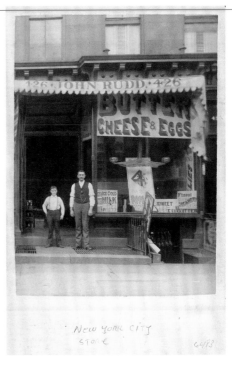

Anonymous
Mr. and Mrs. A. H. Cinch, c. 1860s
Salted paper print mounted on paper
7¾ x 5⁷⁄₁₆"

Turner Studio, Boston
Portrait of a Young Man, c. 1860–1870
Carte-de-viste. Albumen print
mounted on cardboard
3⁷⁄₈ x 2³⁄₈"

S. Marksville Studio, New York
John Rudd, c. 1890
Cabinet card. Albumen print mounted
on cardboard and inscribed
5½ x 4"

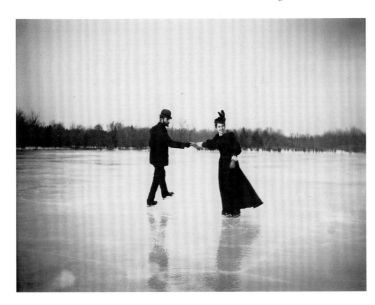

Anonymous
Couple Ice Skating, c. 1890
Gelatin silver print
4¾ x 6³⁄₈"

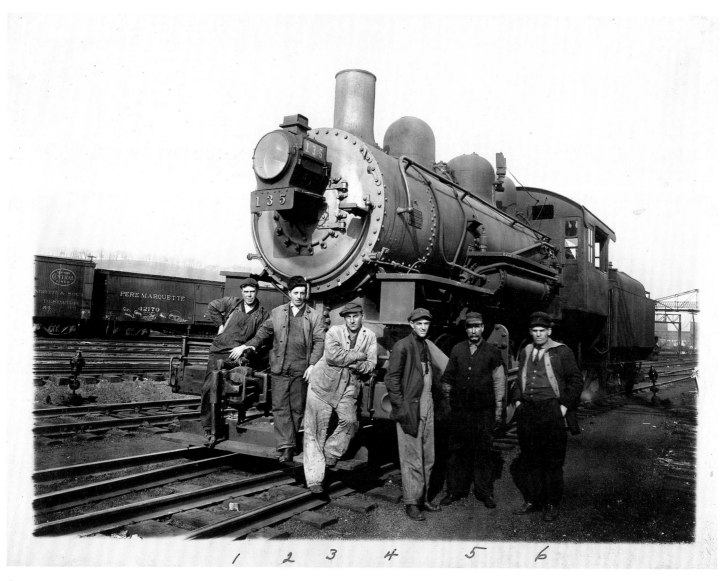

Anonymous
Pere Marquette Railroad Company Crew, 1914
Albumen print mounted on cardboard, inscribed on recto & verso
6½ x 8¾"

This photograph commemorated the reassembling of a six-man locomotive crew in 1914. The numbers below the image serve to identify the crewmen, whose names are handwritten on the back of the card: William Reevau, conductor; George Lettair, brakeman; John Brown, engineer; Joe Kelly, switchman; George Langley, fireman; and Theodore Saululure, brakeman. They stand before Pere Marquette Railroad engine 135, which was retired from duty in 1905. Taken nine years later, this photograph most likely preserves the memory of their work together.

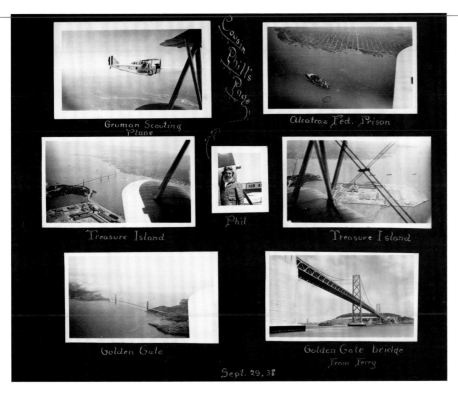

Anonymous
Cousin Phill's Page, Sept. 29, 38, 1938
Gelatin silver prints mounted on paper and inscribed
Approximately 2¾ x 4½" each, with variations

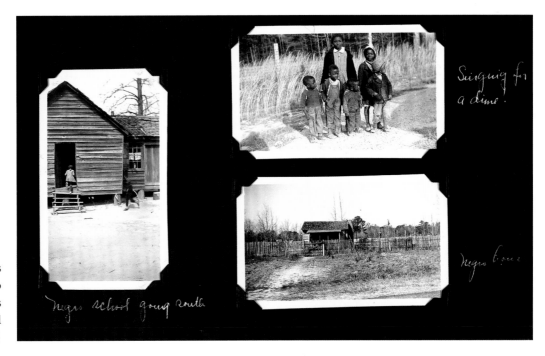

Anonymous
Untitled Album Page, c. 1930
Three gelatin silver prints
mounted on paper and inscribed
2¾ x 4½" (each image)

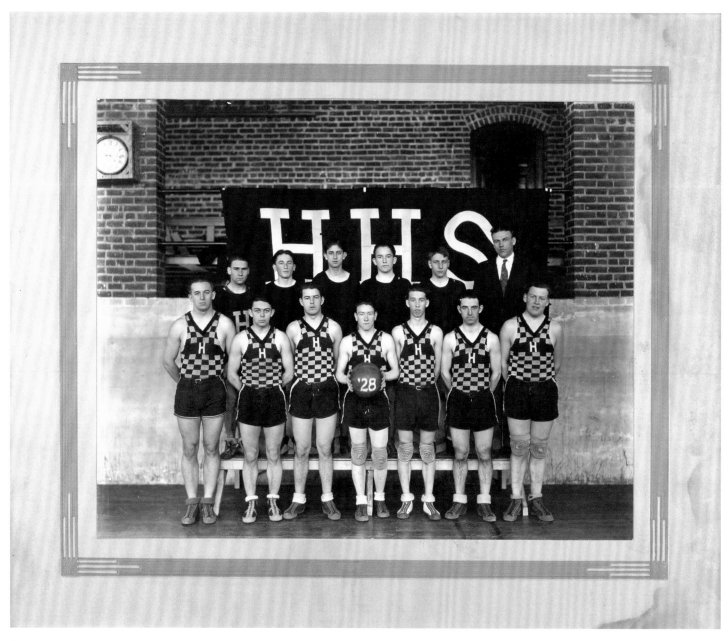

Anonymous
HHS Men's Basketball Team, 1928
Gelatin silver print mounted on cardboard
7½ x 9½"

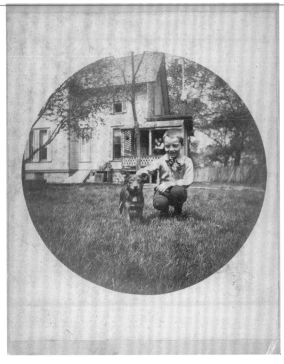

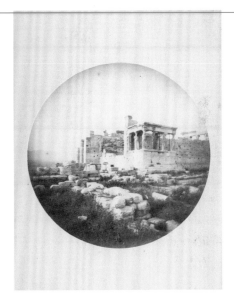

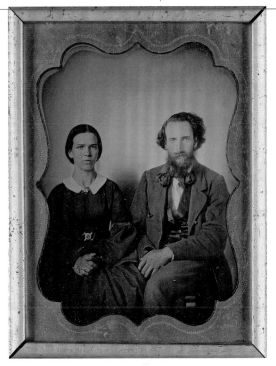

Anonymous
The Erechtheion, c. 1880
Kodak #1 photograph. Albumen
print mounted on cardboard
2½" diameter

Anonymous
Boy with Dog, 1891
Kodak #2 photograph. Collodion printing-out
paper print mounted on cardboard
3½" diameter

Anonymous
Seated Couple, c. 1865
Ambrotype, hand-colored, in original gilt frame
4¾ x 3½"

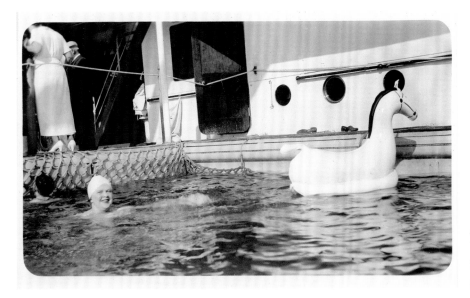

Anonymous
Woman and Inflatable Horse in Pool, c. 1940
Gelatin silver print
3 x 5⅜"

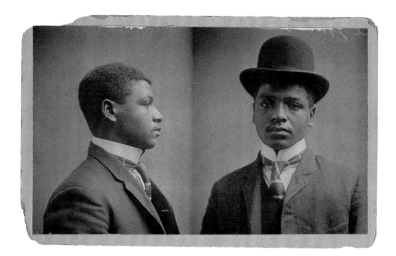

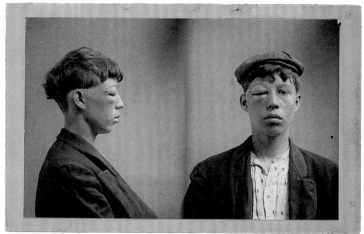

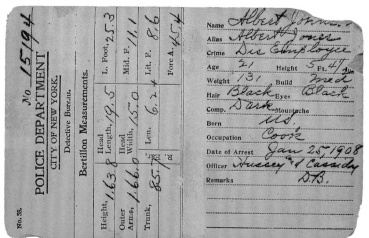

New York City Detective Bureau
Albert Johnson, 1908 (recto & verso)
Bertillon Card. Platinum print mounted on
cardboard, inscribed on verso
3 x 4¹⁵⁄₁₆"

New York City Detective Bureau
Edward Cooper, 1908 (recto & verso)
Bertillon Card. Platinum print mounted on
cardboard, inscribed on verso
2⅞ x 4¾"

The New York City Detective Bureau produced these images of Edward Cooper and Albert Johnson in 1908 as a means to identify repeat offenders and reduce recidivism. These criminal identification cards utilize the system originated at the end of the nineteenth century in Paris by French criminologist Alphonse Bertillon. Known as anthropometry, or Bertillonage, the method relied on detailed bodily measurements (listed on verso) to augment the mugshot and quickly became the standard criminal identification method of the early twentieth century. Bertillon's system was motivated by his fundamental mistrust of the photographic image as a reliable method of identification. Instead he argued that the visual image necessitated supplementary bodily measurements and descriptions to be useful as a detection and archival tool.

PROOF

Proof refers to the ways photographs authenticate experience. In many societies, photographic images serve to validate social customs. Wedding pictures confirm and complete the experience of marriage for its participants. News photographs corroborate the narratives of the journalist's story and confirm events as newsworthy. Insurance and police photographs certify accounts of crimes and calamities.

This function of photography rests in part on the common belief in photographic objectivity: if the photograph is a direct record of its subject, it follows that the photographic image can be used to check the validity of other, less-reliable representations (such as memories, artistic renderings, or even language itself). But using photographs as evidence is also an outgrowth of modern bureaucratic culture, where paperwork (forms, bills, receipts, and images) endorses all sorts of activities in civic and individual contexts. Photographs, for example, are included on identification cards and driver's licenses to prove the identities of their holders.

Woman with Fish, an early color photograph, authenticates the story of a remarkable catch. Long after the tuna in question was eaten or released, this simple snapshot proves the successful capture of an enormous fish. The standard composition of this fishing photograph heightens its legitimacy. Similar to other photographs of its kind, the anonymous fisherwoman here stands next to a vertical, hanging fish. In connecting compositionally with the great body of fisher-and-trophy images, the photograph draws credibility from the familiarity of its format.

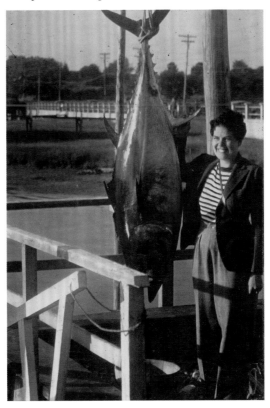

Anonymous
Woman with Fish, c. 1950s
Early chromogenic print
7 x 5"

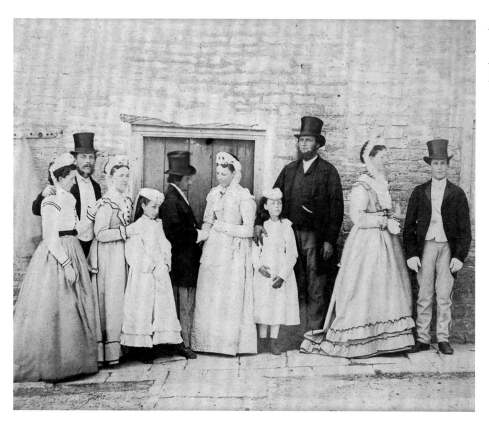

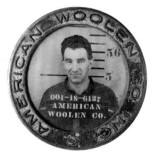

Anonymous
Wedding at North Dorset, c. 1869
Albumen print mounted on cardboard
4⅛ x 5"

Anonymous
American Woolen Co. Inc., c. 1920
Identification badge. Gelatin silver
print and metal badge
1½" diameter

Anonymous
Taken September 1892, 1892
Kodak #2 photograph. Albumen print
mounted on cardboard
3½" diameter

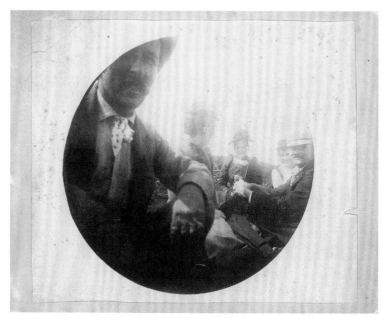

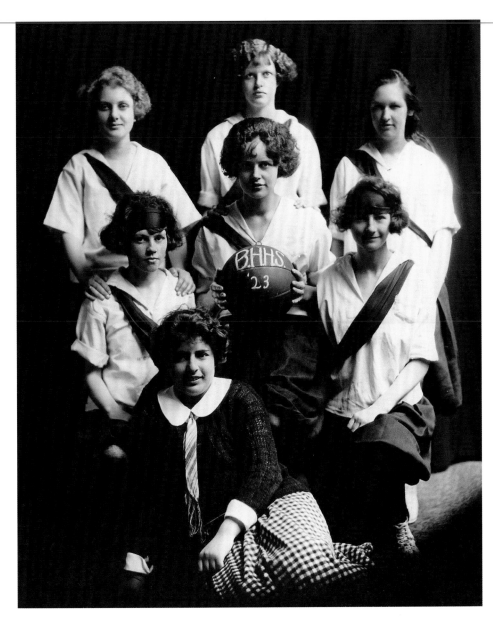

Anonymous
*Bar Harbor High School Women's
Basketball Team*, 1923
Albumen print
8¾ x 7¼"

This team portrait appeared in the 1923 edition of *The Islander*, the yearbook of the now-defunct Bar Harbor High School in Maine, which operated as a coeducational school between 1908 and 1968. Three of the photograph's sitters were members of Bar Harbor's 1923 senior class, and can be identified from portraits elsewhere in *The Islander*. Jessie Walker Stalford ("Jess"), captain of the team between 1921 and 1923, holds a basketball at the center of the portrait; Alice (Evelyn) MacQuinn ("Quinnie") sits to the left of Walker, and Sylvia (Marian) Kurson ("Sis"), team manager, is seated at the bottom. As a yearbook image, *Bar Harbor High School Women's Basketball Team* verifies the participation of several student-athletes, and their dutiful manager, in a successful season: the team had five victories and only one loss in 1923, and nearly won the Maine state championship.

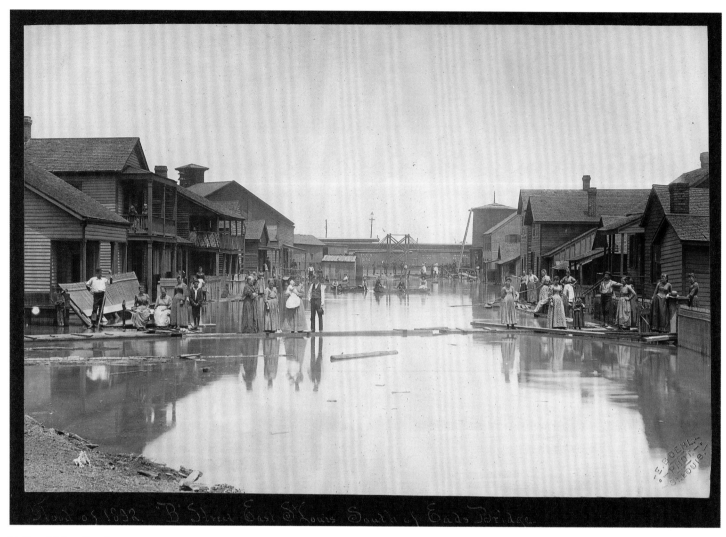

Flood of 1892. "B" Street East St. Louis South of Eads Bridge.

E. Boehl Studio, St. Louis
Flood of 1892. "B" Street East St. Louis South of Eads Bridge, 1892
Albumen print mounted on cardboard and inscribed
6¼ x 9¼"

This photograph of a spring flood was likely taken by the St. Louis, Missouri, photographer Emil Boehl. The low, flat topography of East St. Louis, Illinois (across the Mississippi River from St. Louis, Missouri) made it especially vulnerable to the periodic floods of the Mississippi. At the end of the nineteenth century, East St. Louis was populated largely by recent European immigrants who served as the primary workforce for the massive National Stockyards, a local rail yard (which can be seen in the distance of this image), and a number of nearby factories. With groups of these residents arranged around clapboard homes on makeshift footbridges or floating in rowboats, this photograph certifies the severity of the 1892 flood and charts its disruption of life in East St. Louis.

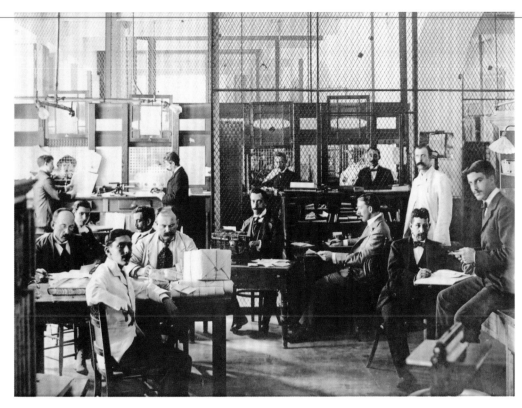

Anonymous
Clerks in Mailroom, c. 1900
Gelatin silver print
5⅞ x 7¾"

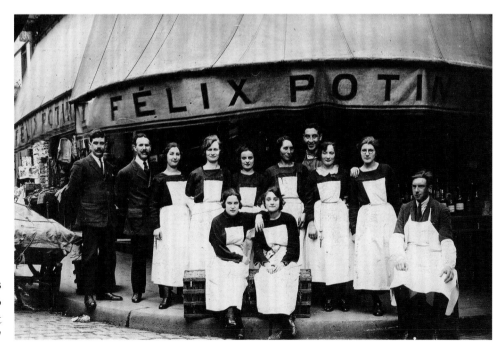

Anonymous
Felix Potin, c. 1910
Gelatin silver print
3½ x 5½"

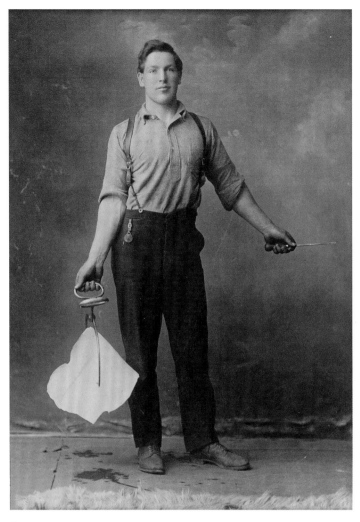

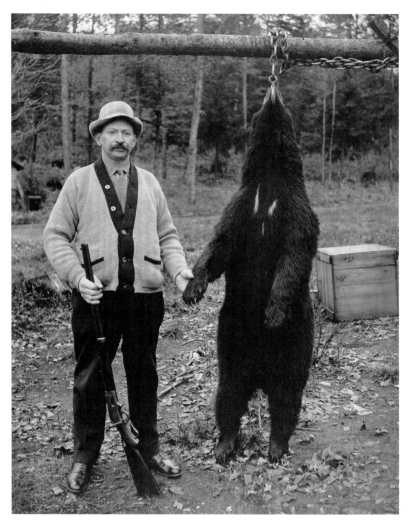

Anonymous
Ice Man, c. 1890
Cabinet card. Gelatin silver print mounted on cardboard
5½ x 4"

Anonymous
Hunter with Bear, c. 1920s
Gelatin silver print
9⅝ x 7¾"

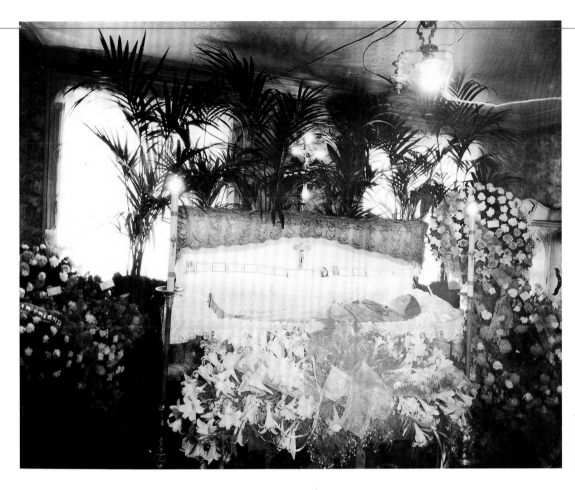

Anonymous
Postmortem Portrait, c. 1920
Gelatin silver print
8 x 10"

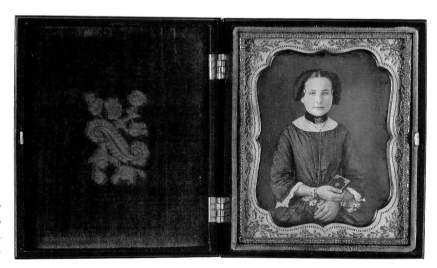

Anonymous
Seated Woman Holding Daguerreotype Case, c. 1850
Daguerreotype, hand-colored, in original case
2¾ x 2⅛"

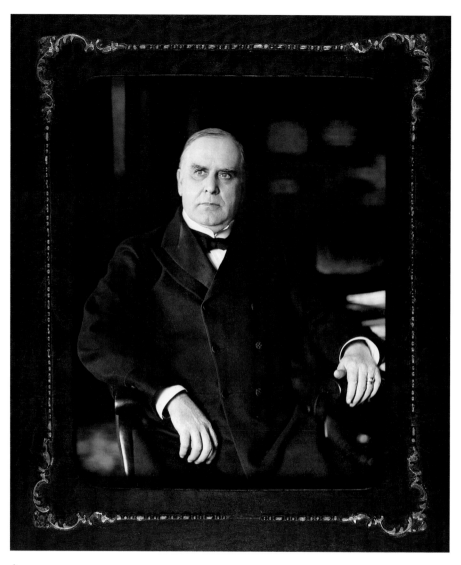

Anonymous
Mourning Portrait of William McKinley, c. 1901
Gelatin silver print in original wood and gilt frame
9½ x 7½"

Having served a tumultuous first term during which he guided the nation through the Spanish-American War, and not long after he began his second term as President, William McKinley was assassinated in 1901 at the Pan-American Exposition in Buffalo. Set in a somber black frame, this mourning portrait was part of a wave of popular memorial imagery that followed his death. The photograph verifies McKinley's presidential identity for posterity. Sitting casually in an armchair, and gazing contemplatively out of the frame, McKinley appears as a comfortable and thoughtful statesman. He is dressed in the formal garb of a tuxedo, reaffirming the genteel political persona he fashioned over his career.

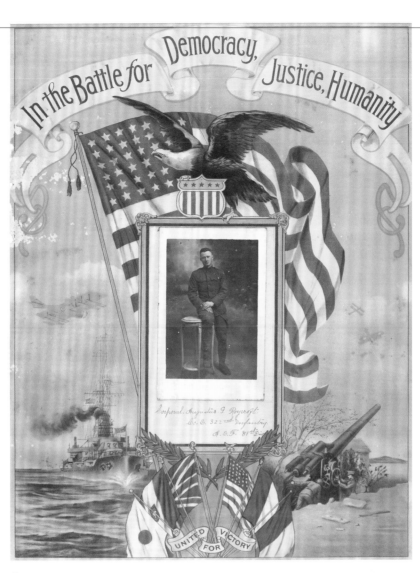

Anonymous
In the Battle for Democracy, Justice, Humanity, 1918
Gelatin silver print affixed to commemorative poster
4½ x 3" (image), 18 x 13½" (poster)

Corporal Augustus Roycroft, photographed in the center, was an infantryman in the 322nd Regiment, 81st Infantry Division in World War I and part of the American Expeditionary Force. The 81st Infantry Division was organized primarily of Southern draftees in August of 1917, and initially stationed at Camp Jackson, South Carolina, before leaving for France in July 1918. The division participated in the brutal Meuse-Argonne Offensive of that year, a successful but bloody effort by American forces to break through the German line. This poster verifies Roycroft's membership in the division and his commitment to the war effort, connecting his likeness to the various patriotic and military vignettes arranged around it.

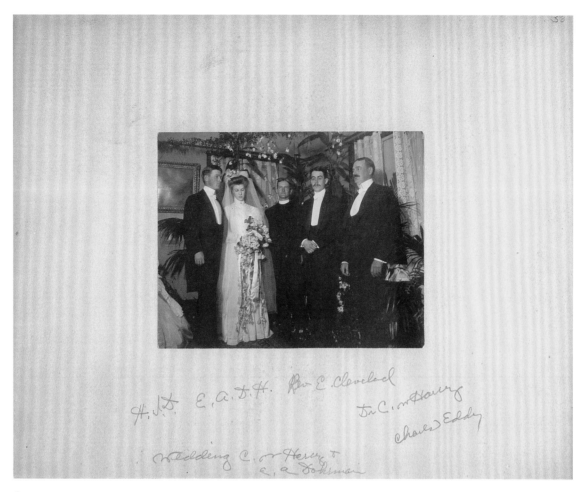

Anonymous
Wedding C. M. Henry & E. A. Dohrman, c. 1890
Albumen print mounted on cardboard and inscribed
3¾ x 4¾"

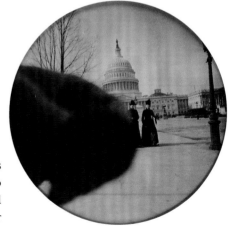

Anonymous
Two Women in front of Capitol Building, c. 1890
Kodak #2 photograph. Albumen print mounted on cardboard
3½" diameter

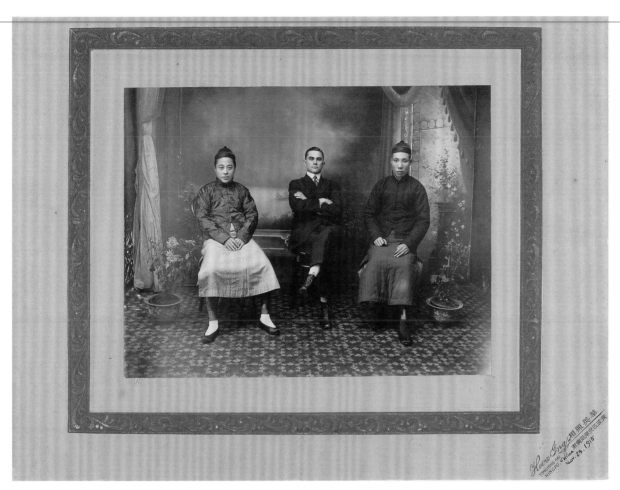

Hwa Ing, Ningpo, China
Remembrance of Our Mutual Friendship, Nov. 23, 1915, 1915
Studio card. Gelatin silver print mounted on cardboard
5⅝ x 7⅜"

Anonymous
Three Portraits, c. 1920
Photographic pocket mirrors.
Celluloid-covered gelatin
silver prints on metal
2¼" diameter each

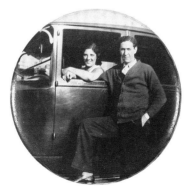
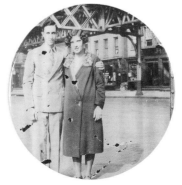
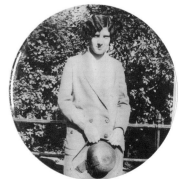

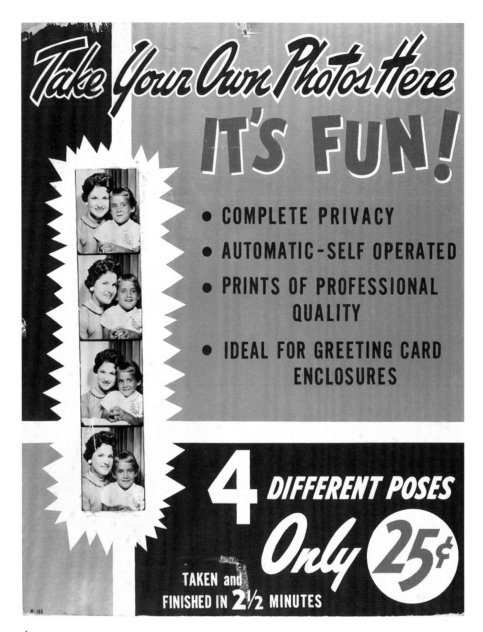

Anonymous
Take Your Own Photos Here, c. 1950–1960
Promotional sign for photo booth with strip of four images
affixed. Gelatin silver print mounted on cardboard
13⅞ x 10¾"

SURROGATE

Surrogate refers to the ways that photographs stand in for lived experience. From its beginnings, people have seen photography as a direct, unmediated mode of representation and a vehicle for recording objective fact. In some cases (and in some cultures) photographs themselves are considered traces of reality—direct indexes of the subject of the image. The photograph functions as a substitute for the "real" moment of experience it depicts.

With the expansion of the photography market over the course of the late nineteenth and early twentieth centuries, specialized modes of photographic production developed to accompany and embellish all manner of social life. Photographic portraits of the deceased were created and are valued as relics of their lost subjects. Travel photography provides vacationers with inexpensive keepsakes to remember their journeys. It also offers visions of distant places to the armchair traveler. News photography provides glimpses of the horrors of war and calamity without the danger of actual physical involvement.

Masked Ballerina presents a titillating depiction of the female body for late-nineteenth-century viewers. Images of the "ballerina" were understood in highly sexualized terms at the time, often serving as a surrogate for the prostitute. The exposed legs and midriff, as well as the way the model hides her face—and identity—with the mask reaffirms the salacious nature of the image. This image is a single example of one of photography's most salient modern industries: the production and circulation of erotica. By their nature, erotic images serve as substitutes for human intimacy and are designed to provide viewers with a pleasurable experience of physical desire.

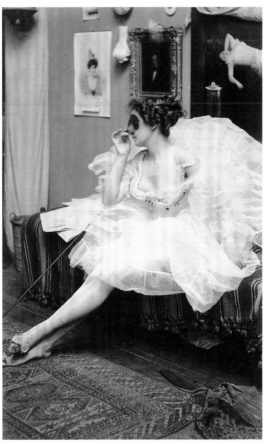

Anonymous
Masked Ballerina, c. 1880
Albumen print
7^{11}/$_{16}$ x 4^{3}⁄$_{4}$"

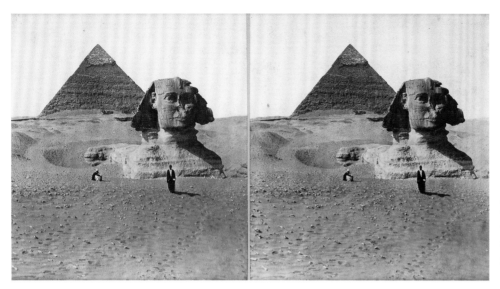

Frank M. Good Studio, London
Egypt—The Second Pyramid and Sphinx, c. 1860s
Stereograph. Albumen prints
mounted on cardboard
3³⁄₁₆ x 3" (each image)

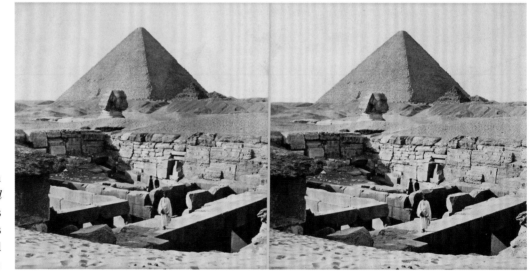

Frank M. Good Studio, London
*Egypt—The Great Pyramid and Excavated
Temple*, c. 1860s
Stereograph. Albumen prints
mounted on cardboard
3³⁄₁₆ x 3" (each image)

Frank M. Good Studio, London
Egypt—Pyramid of Dashoor, c. 1860s
Stereograph. Albumen prints
mounted on cardboard
3³⁄₁₆ x 3" (each image)

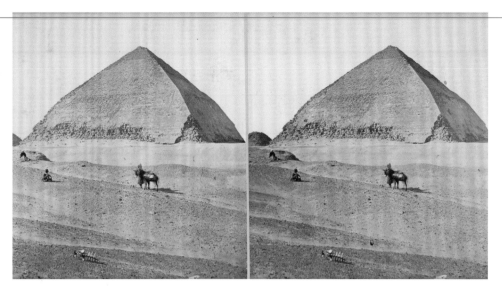

Frank M. Good Studio, London
*Jerusalem—View in the Garden
of Gethsemane*, c. 1860s
Stereograph. Albumen prints
mounted on cardboard
3³⁄₁₆ x 3" (each image)

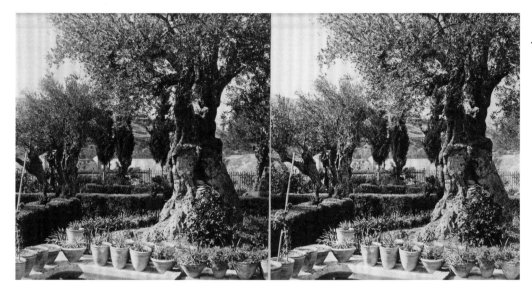

These stereographs were photographed and published by Frank M. Good, a London photographer who produced stereo views in thematic series for European and American audiences. These images were part of Good's "Eastern Series," a popular collection of about 250 scenes of Egypt and the Holy Land. When viewed with a stereoscope (or stereo viewer), these images offered an illusionistic stand-in for a trip to the sites of antiquity. The goal was to give the viewer the impression of actually "being there" in the scene.

The dazzling effect of the stereo card is produced by the juxtaposition of two similar images taken from slightly different angles, which correspond to the position of the viewer's eyes. When viewed at an appropriate distance, the two images are collapsed perceptually into one seemingly three-dimensional scene. Filling the viewer's entire field of vision, the stereographic format further intensifies the photograph's simulation of reality.

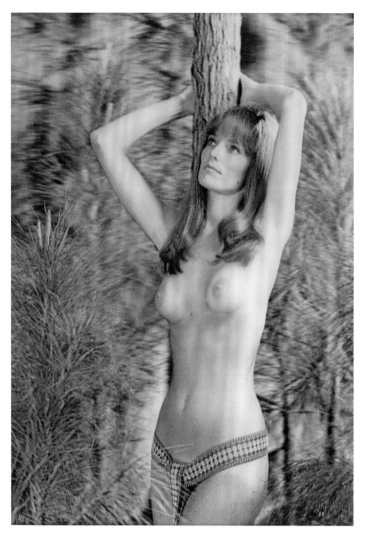

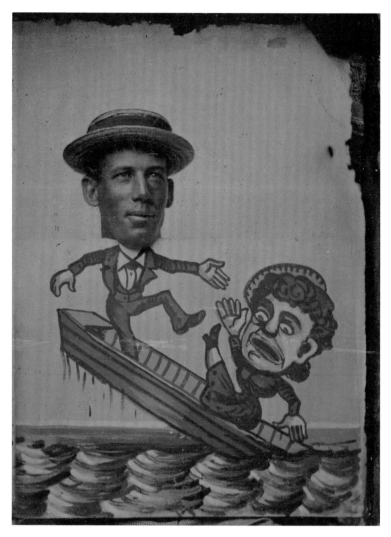

Anonymous
Nature Beauty, c. 1970
Lenticular postcard
6½ x 4⅝"

Anonymous
Man with Carnival Cutout, c. 1900
Tintype
3½ x 2⅝"

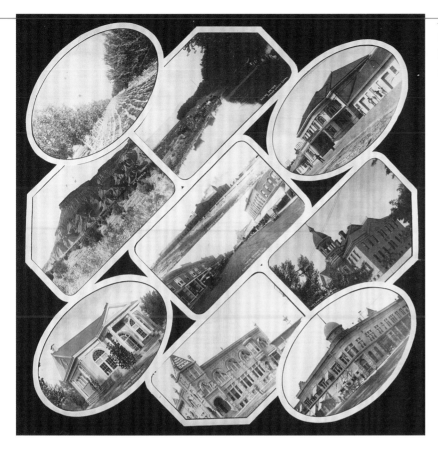

Anonymous
Grand Junction, Colorado, c. 1930
Photographic bandana. Cyanotype on fabric
17 x 17½"

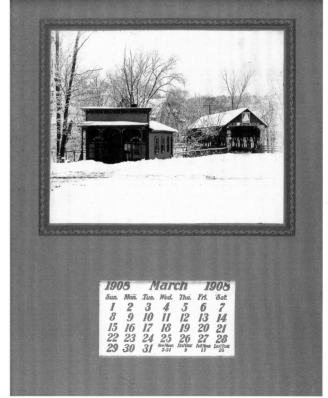

Anonymous
Collins Calendar Card, 1908
Gelatin silver print mounted on
cardboard with paper calendar
4 x 5"

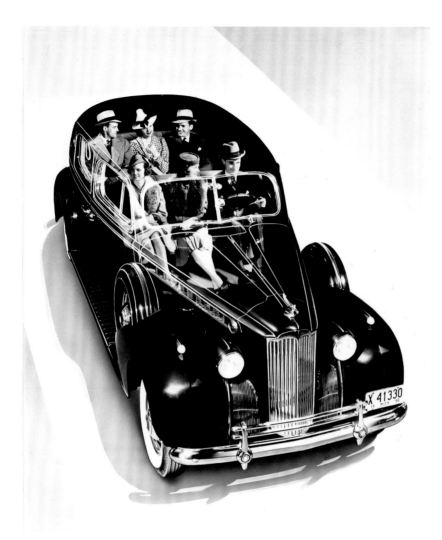

Anonymous
Packard Automobile, Michigan, 1940
Gelatin silver print
9⅞ x 7⅞"

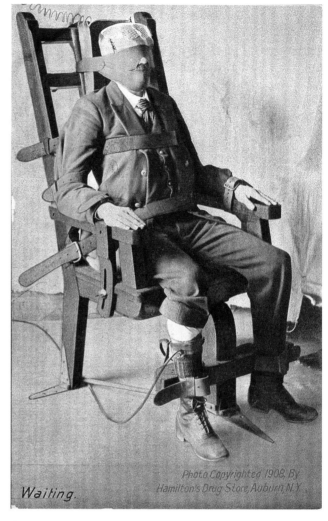

Anonymous
Waiting, 1908
Color photolithograph
3½ x 5½"

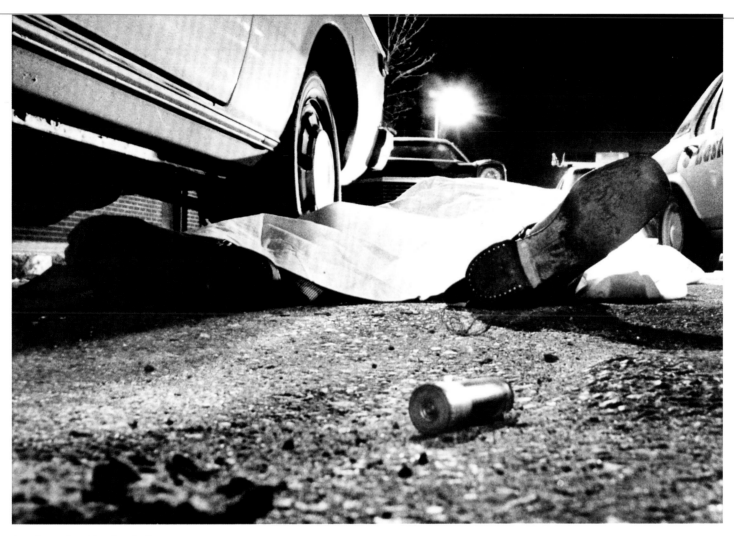

Attributed to Stanley J. Forman
Gunned Down, c. 1970
Gelatin silver print
8¾ x 12¼"

The origin of *Gunned Down* is believed to be the files of the *Boston Herald*, in the "General News" section. The headline on the back of the photograph reads: "Shot gun shell lies at man's feet after he was shot and killed while in an argument in East Boston." Photographed from the ground level, the image combines the formality of crime scene photography with the spur-of-the-moment quality of journalism. The photographer pushes the crude details of the scene, the shell casing and the dead man's shoes, to the foreground, revealing a contemporary approach to the photographic documentation of street violence. Although the image is attributed to former *Herald* staff photographer and three-time Pulitzer Prize winner Stanley J. Forman, this attribution cannot be confirmed.

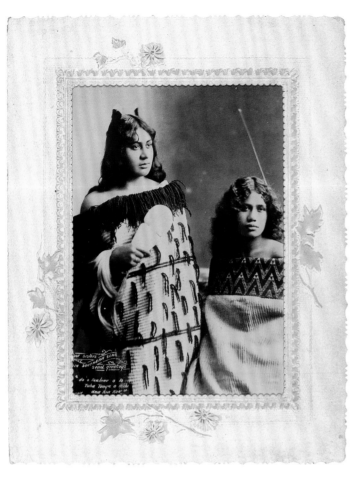

Anonymous
*Your Sisters in Southern Seas Send
Greetings*, 1902 (exterior & interior)
Gelatin silver print and paper card,
inscribed on interior
5⅞ x 4⅛"

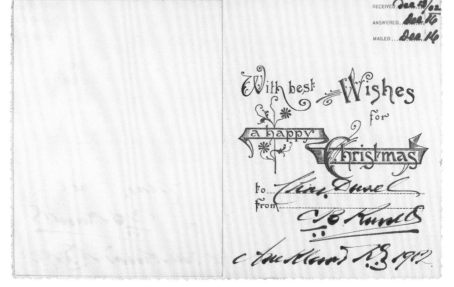

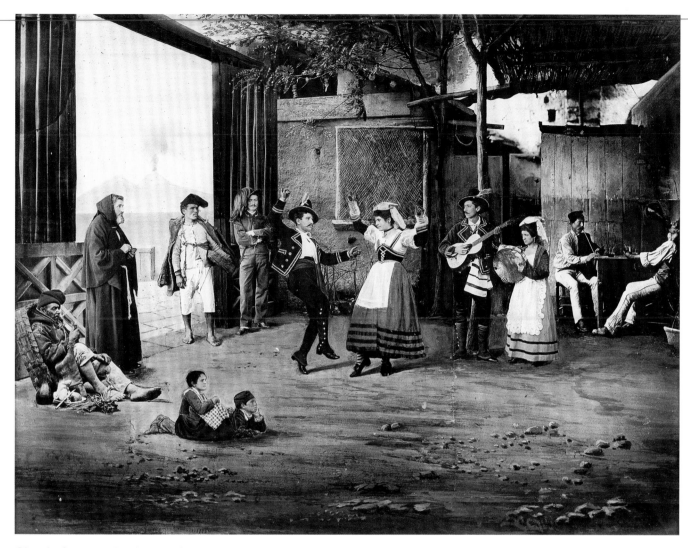

Giorgio Sommer Studio, Naples
The Tarantella, Naples, 1875
Albumen print, hand-colored
7¾ x 9¹⁵⁄₁₆"

The German-born photographer Giorgio Sommer established a studio in Naples in 1857 that specialized in the production of souvenir images of Neapolitan life and culture. This depiction of the Tarantella (a traditional dance) is a hand-colored albumen print of a photomontage in which several individual photographs are pasted onto a hand-drawn scene, complete with a schematic Vesuvius smoking in the distance. Two of the figures are repeated several times in the scene: for example, the dancing male figure at center reappears as a musician at the right. Colorful and constructed, this montage condensed a complex Neapolitan tradition into an easily digested photographic fantasy of festivity, indolence, and intemperance that was successful with photographic consumers.

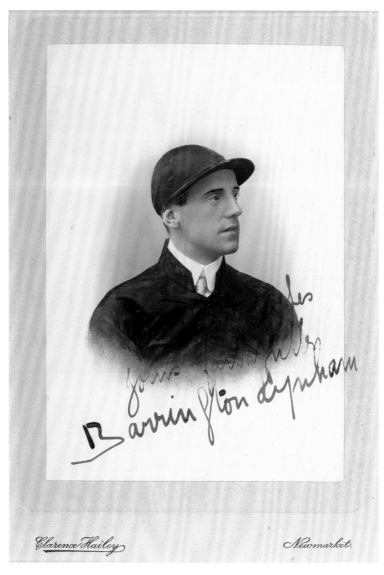

Clarence Hailey
Barrington Lynham, c. 1907
Gelatin silver print, hand-colored, mounted on cardboard
5¾ x 4"

Barrington Lynham was a jockey in England at the turn of the twentieth century. He rode the horse Witch Elm to victory in the 1000 Guineas Stakes at Newmarket in 1907, and rode another stakes winner in 1910. There is a street named after him in Newmarket Suffolk, as well as a race in France, the "Prix Barry Lynham," demonstrating that he was an athlete of some notoriety at the time. This boldly hand-colored studio portrait of Lynham was probably circulated as a popular collectible, somewhat like the modern baseball trading card.

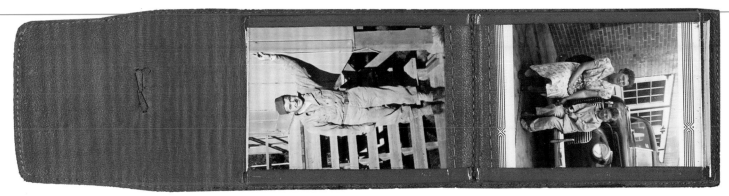

Anonymous
World War II Soldier's Pocket Album, c. 1943 (interior & exterior)
Pocket album. Gelatin silver prints in leather folio
3 x 2¼" (each image)

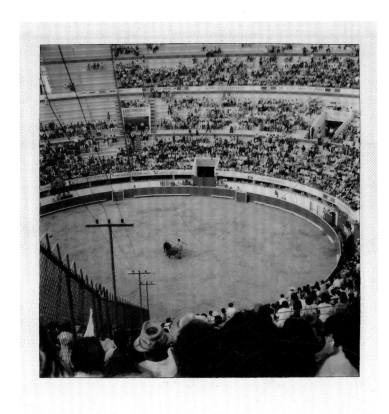

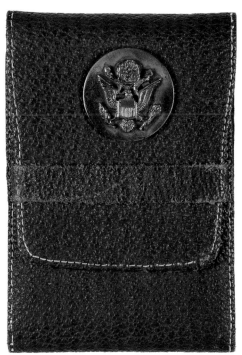

Anonymous
Bullfight, c. 1970s
Polaroid SX-70 photograph
3⅛ x 3⅛"

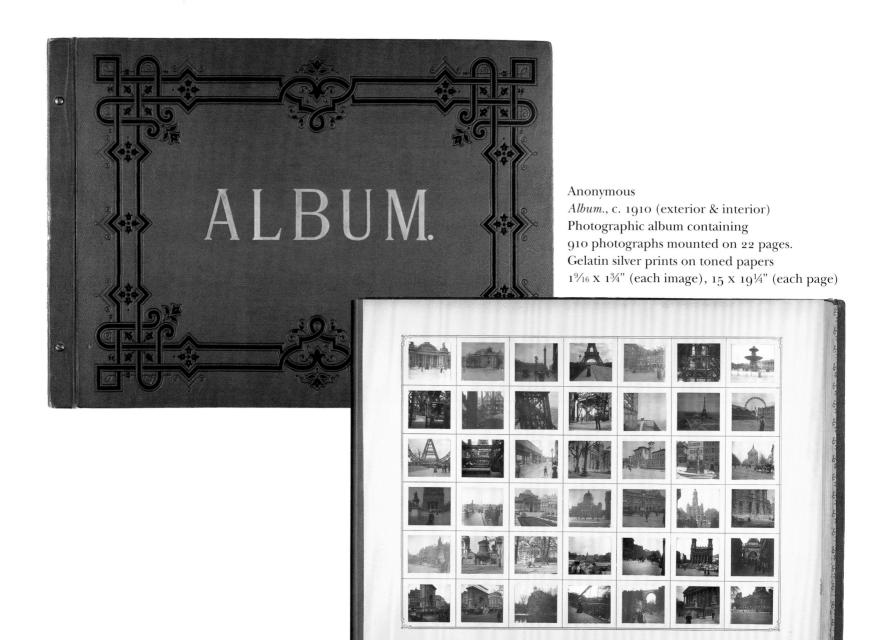

Anonymous
Album., c. 1910 (exterior & interior)
Photographic album containing
910 photographs mounted on 22 pages.
Gelatin silver prints on toned papers
1⁹⁄₁₆ x 1¾" (each image), 15 x 19¼" (each page)

The *Album* includes 22 pages of small, square photographs (910 total) each on a different color of toned paper. The photographs depict popular European sites, and document a Grand Tour undertaken by the richly dressed woman pictured in the foreground throughout the album. The open page includes several images of popular European tourist sites, including the Eiffel Tower and the Tuileries Gardens in Paris. Each page is organized with a different, hand-stenciled grid inside a delicate, printed gold border. A standout photographic album, the technical or commercial origins of the colored photographs and the album's format remain unknown.

YARDSTICK

Yardstick refers to the ways photographs are used to evaluate, measure, and study reality. As scientific inquiry evolved beyond the boundaries of the immediately seen or experienced, new photographic processes (X-rays, micrographs, and astronomical photos) offered access to areas of bodily, natural, and cosmic function previously unseen by the naked eye. These "hidden" realities—a living human skeleton, cell structures of plants, distant galaxies—could be understood and analyzed through photographic representations.

The *Photographische Sternkarten* (Photographic Star Chart) was one such scientific photographic effort. It was made to map and measure the positions of stars and heavenly bodies in a small section of space. The flexibility of photographic processes allowed astron-omers to reverse an image's tonalities, producing a more legible negative print of the section studied.

Scientific photography is only one aspect of a longstanding interest in using the photograph as a comparative tool. Grammar and secondary schools generate yearly pictures of their classes, allowing parents to chart the progress of their children through school and life. Militaries use photographs to analyze potential targets for attacks and to measure the success of completed campaigns. The advertising industry is based on offering photographic images of happy customers and useful products as standards against which potential consumers might measure their own identities, financial circumstances, and success.

Johann Palisa und Max Wolf
Photographische Sternkarten, March 6, 1902, 1902
Gelatin silver print
$14^{3}/_{16}$ x $10^{1}/_{16}$"

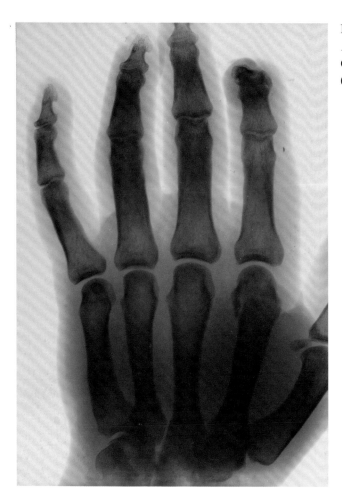

Drake Brothers Studio
X-ray of a Human Hand, c. 1900
Gelatin silver print mounted on cardboard
6 $^{11}/_{16}$ x 4 $^{5}/_{8}$"

Anonymous
Construction of the Panama Canal,
c. 1904–1914
Stereograph. Gelatin silver print
mounted on cardboard
3¼ x 3" (each image)

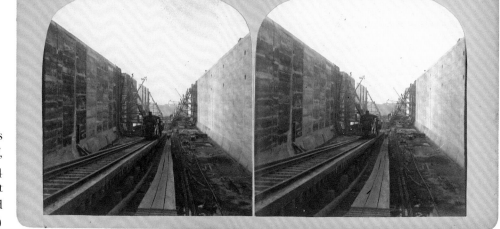

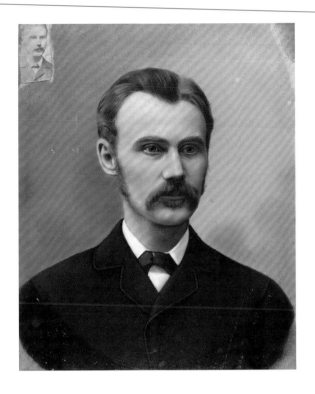

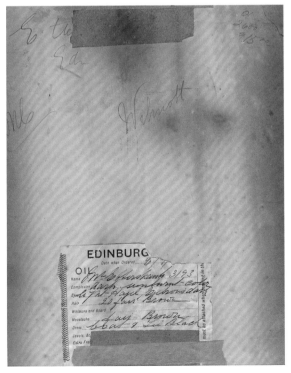

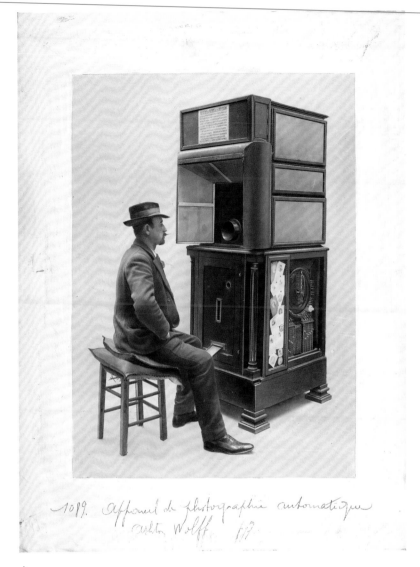

Anonymous
Photo Booth Advertisement 1089, c. 1910
Gelatin silver print mounted on cardboard and inscribed
9½ x 6⅞"

Anonymous
Dual Portrait, 1870–1880 (recto & verso)
Albumen print affixed to hand-painted solar enlargement
and cardboard, inscribed label on verso: label lists
physical description of subject
2⅜ x 1⅜"

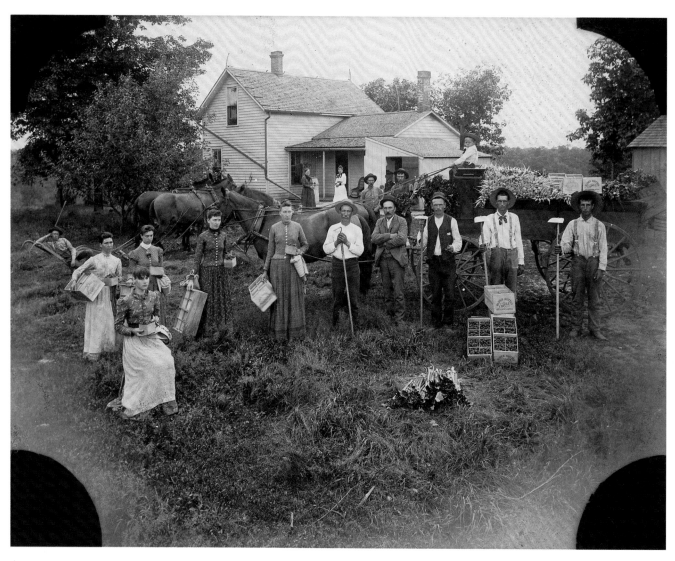

Anonymous
Oliver Dutton Grower, Ottumwa, Iowa, 1880
Albumen print
$7\frac{7}{8}$ x 10"

Oliver Dutton Grower was one of several large commercial farms in and around Ottumwa, Iowa. Ottumwa was settled in 1844, but became a manufacturing, farming, and transportation hub in the 1870s with the extension of several railroad lines through the town. Like many local growers, Oliver Dutton supplied eastern markets with produce. This photograph, with its edges masked during the printing process to hide a faulty lens, provides a visual inventory of a successful farming operation, combining employees, equipment, physical plant, and products in one image of prosperity.

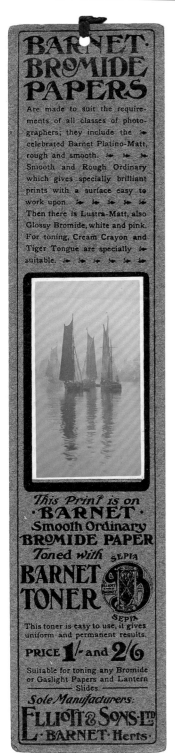

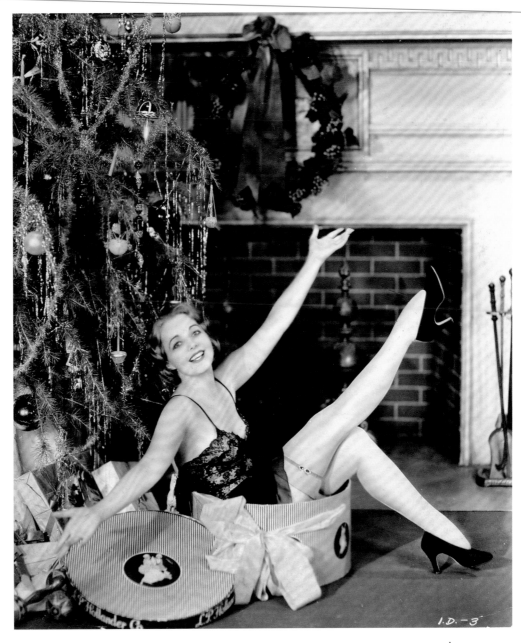

Anonymous
L. P. Hollander Co. Christmas Photograph, c. 1930
Gelatin silver print
8½ x 7¼"

Anonymous
Barnet Bromide Papers, c. 1910
Promotional bookmark. Gelatin silver-bromide print
mounted on paper with red ribbon attached
2¼ x 1¼" (image) 8⅜ x 1¾" (paper)

79

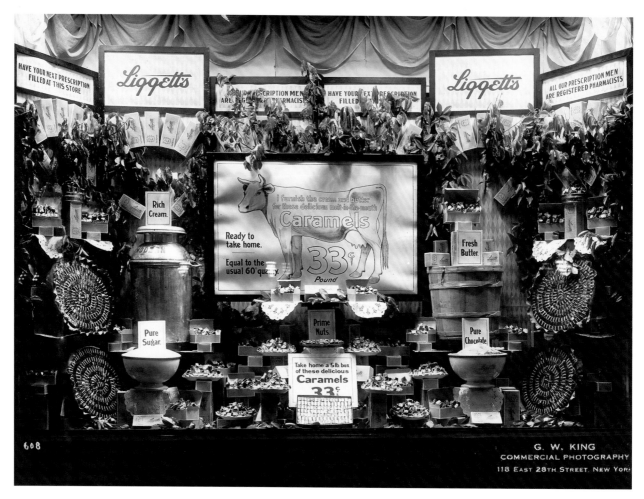

G. W. King, New York
Liggett's Window Display, c. 1920
Gelatin silver print
8 x 10"

Tom Kelley Studios
Golden Dreams, 1954–1955, photographed in 1949
Color half-tone mounted on cardboard
© Tom Kelley Studios
10 x 8" (image) 17 x 10" (cardboard)

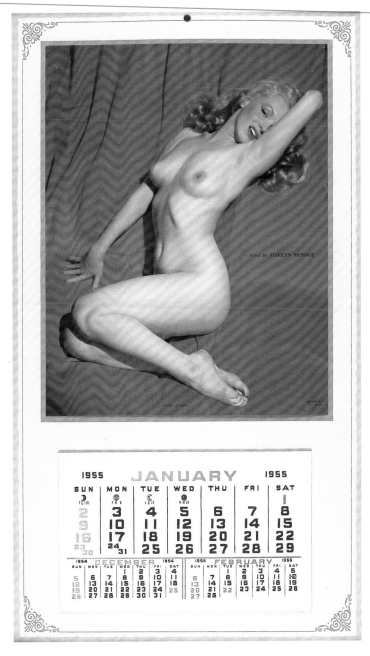

Golden Dreams is an unauthorized version of photographer Tom Kelly's infamous calendar that featured a nude image of the beautiful, young, then-unknown Marilyn Monroe. Brown & Bigelow of Chicago published Kelly's original "Red Velvet" image, depicting an outstretched Monroe basking on a red velvet background, as a promotional calendar in 1952. The following year, the photograph served as the inaugural centerfold for a new men's magazine called *Playboy*. This version of the calendar is most likely a later counterfeit of Kelly's original, published without the photographer's permission.

81

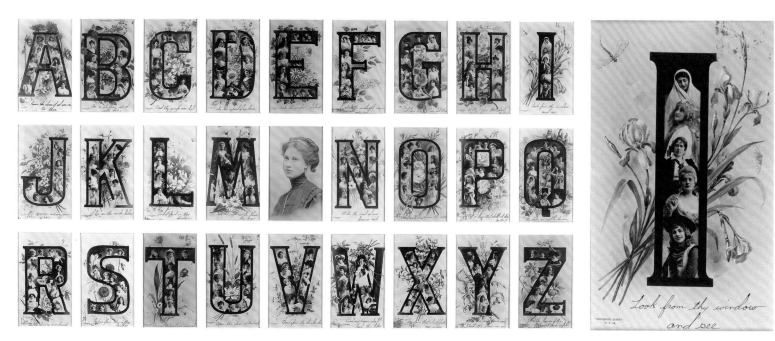

Anonymous and the Rotograph Company, New York
Alphabet Montage, 1904 (with detail)
Twenty-six real-photo postcards with one photographic portrait
in center. Gelatin silver bromide prints, inscribed
5 x 3" (each card)

Each card in this *Alphabet Montage* was sent over the course of several days in 1904 to the anonymous female sitter of the portrait at center. Alphabetic postcards were popular at the turn of the twentieth century. The Rotograph Company in New York published this set of cards. The 26 real-photo postcards, each of which features several images of women organized within the card's specific letter, are hand-inscribed with verses from Bayard Taylor's (1825–1878) poem "Bedouin Song," originally published in his *Poems of the Orient* of 1854. Though its romantic flourishes were dated by 1904, Taylor's poem was appropriate for a message sent to a distant loved one. Taylor, a foreign correspondent for the *Saturday Evening Post*, the *United States Gazette*, and the *New York Tribune*, produced most of his popular poetry and prose while traveling.

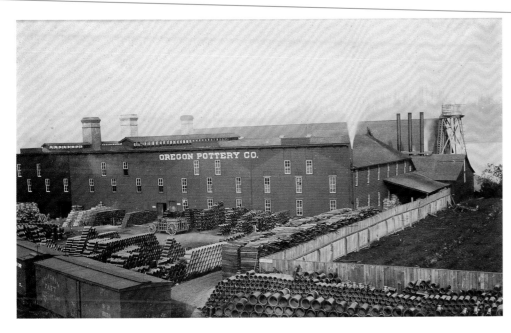

Anonymous
Oregon Pottery Co., Before and After, 1890
Two albumen prints
4¼ x 7" (each image)

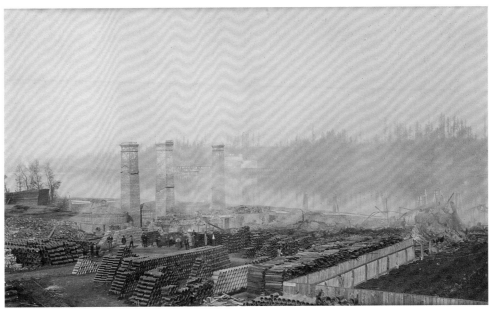

These two albumen prints were made before and after the fire at the Oregon Pottery factory in Portland, Oregon, in 1890. Built on the Willamette River in 1882, the factory was the latest and most modern manufacturing facility of the Oregon Pottery Company, founded in 1866 by Freeman Smith in Buena Vista, Oregon. The identical vantage points of these photographs strengthen their function as documentation of the effects of the catastrophe: details of the surrounding landscape, stacks of masonry pipe, the angling wooden fence, and the three stone smokestacks appear in both photographs in nearly identical positions.

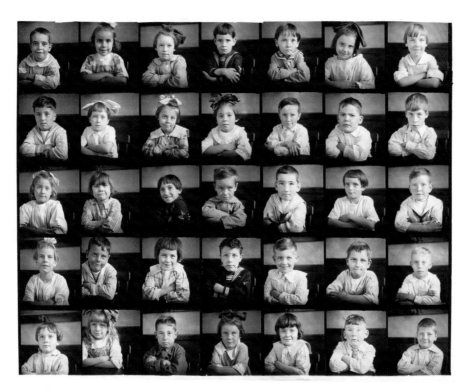

Anonymous
1st Grade Bruce School, W. Lynn, Mass,
November 1921, 1921 (recto & verso)
Contact sheet. Gelatin silver print,
inscribed on verso
7⅜ x 9⁷⁄₁₆"

BIBLIOGRAPHY

The Vernacular Precedent and Theories of Visual Culture

Appadurai, Arjun. *The Social Life of Things: Commodities in Cultural Perspective.* Cambridge and New York: Cambridge University Press, 1986.

Attfield, Judy. *Wild Things: The Material Culture of Everyday Life.* Oxford: Berg, 2000.

Carter, Thomas, and Bernard L. Herman, eds. *Perspectives in Vernacular Architecture.* Columbia, MO: University of Missouri Press, 1989.

Dyer, Richard. *White.* London and New York: Routledge, 1997.

Grosz, Elizabeth A. *Volatile Bodies: Toward a Corporeal Feminism.* Bloomington: Indiana University Press, 1994.

Herman, Bernard L. *Town House: Architecture and Material Life in the Early American City, 1780–1830.* Chapel Hill: University of North Carolina Press, 2005.

———. *The Stolen House.* Charlottesville: University Press of Virginia, 1992.

Hollander, Stacy C., and Brooke Davis Anderson. *American Anthem: Masterworks from the American Folk Art Museum.* New York: Abrams, 2001.

Jones, Amelia, ed. *The Feminism and Visual Culture Reader.* London and New York: Routledge, 2003.

Kouwenhoven, John A. *Made in America: The Arts in Modern American Civilization.* New York: Doubleday, 1948.

———. *Half a Truth is Better Than None: Some Unsystematic Conjectures about Art, Disorder, and American Experience.* Chicago: University of Chicago Press, 1982.

Latour, Bruno. *We Have Never Been Modern.* Cambridge: Harvard University Press, 1993.

Maresca, Frank, and Roger Ricco. *American Vernacular: New Discoveries in Folk, Self-Taught, and Outsider Sculpture.* Boston: Little, Brown, 2002.

Meskell, Lynn. *Object Worlds in Ancient Egypt: Material Biographies Past and Present.* Oxford and New York: Berg, 2004.

Miller, Daniel, ed. *Home Possessions: Material Culture Behind Closed Doors.* Oxford and New York: Berg, 2001.

Mirzoeff, Nicholas. *The Visual Culture Reader.* London: Routledge, 1998.

Prown, Jules. "The Truth of Material Culture: History or Fiction?" In *American Artifacts: Essays in Material Culture.* East Lansing, MI: Michigan State University Press, 2000.

Rapoport, Amos. "The Nature and Definition of the Field." In *House Form and Culture.* Englewood Cliffs, NJ: Prentice Hall, 1969.

Rose, Gillian. *Visual Methodologies: An Introduction to the Interpretation of Visual Materials.* London and Thousand Oaks, CA: Sage, 2001.

Shields, David S. *Civil Tongues & Polite Letters in British America.* Chapel Hill: University of North Carolina Press, 1997.

Stewart, Susan. *On Longing: Narratives of the Miniature, the Gigantic, the Souvenir, the Collection.* Durham: Duke University Press, 1993.

St. George, Robert Blair. *Conversing by Signs: Poetics of Implication in Colonial New England Culture.* Chapel Hill: University of North Carolina Press, 1998.

Sturken, Marita, and Lisa Cartwright. *Practices of Looking: An Introduction to Visual Culture.* Oxford and New York: Oxford University Press, 2001.

Taylor, Charles. *Modern Social Imaginaries.* Durham: Duke University Press, 2004.

Upton, Dell, and John Michael Vlach. *Common Places: Readings in American Vernacular Architecture.* Athens: University of Georgia Press, 1986.

Wertkin, Gerard C., and Lee Kogan. *Encyclopedia of American Folk Art.* New York: Routledge, 2004.

The Vernacular Alternative and Other Models of Photographic History

Afterimage 29, no. 6 (May-June 2002). [Issue on vernacular photography.]

American Art 21, no. 3 (Fall 2007). [Issue on American histories of photography.]

Barthes, Roland. *Camera Lucida: Reflections on Photography*. New York: Farrar, Straus and Giroux, Hill and Wang, 1981.

Batchen, Geoffrey. "Vernacular Photographies." In *Each Wild Idea: Writing, Photography, History*. Cambridge: MIT Press, 2001. [Edited reprint of the 2000 essay.]

————. "Vernacular Photographies," *History of Photography* 24, no. 3 (Autumn 2000): 262–271. [Issue on vernacular photography.]

Bourdieu, Pierre. *Photography: A Middlebrow Art*. Stanford: Stanford University Press, 1990.

Coleman, A. D. "Quotidian or Vernacular Photography: Premises, functions and contexts," *Impact of Science on Society* 42, no. 4 (1992): 315–327.

Edwards, Elizabeth, and Janice Hart, eds. *Photographs Objects Histories: On the Materiality of Images*. London: Routledge, 2004.

Elkins, James. *Photography Theory*. The Art Seminar, 2. New York: Routledge, 2007.

————. "What Do We Want Photography to Be? A Response to Michael Fried," *Critical Inquiry* 31, no. 4 (Summer 2005): 938–956.

Frizot, Michel, ed. *A New History of Photography*. Cologne: Könemann, 1998.

Kaplan, Daile. "Pop Photographica in Everyday Life, 1842–1968," *The Photo Review* 21 (Fall 1998): 2–14.

Lemagny, Jean-Claude, and André Rouillé, eds. *A History of Photography: Social and Cultural Perspectives*. Cambridge and New York: Cambridge University Press, 1987.

Malcolm, Janet. *Diana & Nikon: Essays on the Aesthetic of Photography*. Boston: David R. Godine, 1980.

Marien, Mary Warner. *Photography: A Cultural History*. Upper River Saddle, NJ: Prentice Hall, 2002.

Moore, Kevin D. *Jacques Henri Lartigue: The Invention of an Artist*. Princeton: Princeton University Press, 2004.

Nickel, Douglas R. "History of Photography: The State of the Research," *The Art Bulletin* 83, no. 3 (September 2001): 548–558.

Olin, Margaret. "Touching Photographs: Roland Barthes's 'Mistaken' Identification," *Representations* 80 (Fall 2002): 99–118.

Roberts, John. *The Art of Interruption: Realism, Photography, and the Everyday*. Manchester and New York: Manchester University Press, 1998.

Sontag, Susan. *On Photography*. New York: Farrar, Straus and Giroux, 1973.

Trachtenberg, Alan. *Reading American Photographs: Images as History, Mathew Brady to Walker Evans*. New York: Hill and Wang, 1989.

Williamson, Glenn. "The Getty Research Institute: Materials for a New Photo History," *History of Photography* 22 (Spring 1998): 31–39.

Exhibitions of Vernacular Photography

Batchen, Geoffrey. *Forget Me Not: Photography and Remembrance*. New York: Princeton Architectural Press, 2004.

————. *Photography's Objects*. Albuquerque, NM: University of New Mexico Art Museum, 1997.

Browner, Ann. *Evidence: Photography and Site*. Columbus, OH: Wexner Center for the Arts, The Ohio State University, 1997.

Deitcher, David. *Dear Friends: American Photographs of Men Together 1840–1918*. New York: Harry N. Abrams, 2001.

Fineman, Mia. *Other Pictures: Anonymous Photographs from the Thomas Walter Collection*. Albuquerque, NM: Twin Palms Publishers, 2000.

Germain, Julian. *Brief Encounter*. Salford, England: Salford City Council, 1995.

Glenn, Constance, and John Upton. *The Photograph As Artifice: An Exhibition*. Long Beach: Art Galleries, California State University, Long Beach, 1978.

Hall, Michael, and Shirley Teresa Wajda. *Family Album: The James Rutkowski Collection of American Photographs*. Columbus, OH: Columbus Museum of Art, 2004.

Hines, Babette. *Photobooth*. New York: Princeton Architectural Press, 2002.

Jaguaribe, Claudia. *Anonymous Portraits*. São Paulo: Museo de Arte São Paulo, 1997.

Kaplan, Daile. *Pop Photographica: Photography's Objects in Everyday Life, 1842–1969.* Toronto: Art Gallery of Ontario, 2003.

Lamunière, Michelle, Kate Palmer, and Julia Dolan. *A New Kind of Historical Evidence: Photographs from the Carpenter Center Collection.* Cambridge: Harvard University Art Museums, 2005.

Lokuta, Donald P., and Robert Yoskowitz. *Click!: The Marvelous in American Vernacular Photography.* Trenton, NJ: New Jersey State Museum, 2000.

Miller, Margaret A., Rodger Kingston, and Virginia Heckert. *The Amazing & the Immutable.* Tampa, FL: USF Contemporary Art Museum, 2004.

Norfleet, Barbara P. *Wedding.* New York: Simon and Schuster, 1979.

Patton, Mary. *Pasadena Photographs and Photographers 1880–1915.* Pasadena, CA: Pasadena Historical Society, 1982.

Waldie, D. J. *Close to Home: An American Album.* Los Angeles: J. Paul Getty Museum, 2004.

Wallis, Brian, and Deborah Willis. *African American Vernacular Photography: Selections from the Daniel Cowin Collection.* New York: International Center of Photography, 2005.

White, Stephen, and Andreas Blühm. *The Photograph and the American Dream 1840–1940.* Amsterdam: Van Gogh Museum, distributed in the United States by Distributed Art Publishers, New York, 2001.

Wright, David. "Photography: Questions about the Vernacular," *The New Criterion* 8 (October 1989): 46–50.

Vernacular Collecting, Collections, and Collectors

Allen, James. *Without Sanctuary: Lynching Photography in America.* Santa Fe, NM: Twin Palms, 2000.

The American Image: Photographs from the National Archives, 1860–1960. With an introduction by Alan Trachtenberg. New York: Pantheon Books, 1979.

Badger, Gerry. *Collecting Photography.* London: Mitchell Beazley, 2003.

Bailey, Susan. "A Brief History of Postcard Collecting," *Piecework* 6 (November-December 1998): 14.

Baldwin, Gordon. *Looking at Photographs: A Guide to Technical Terms.* Malibu: J. Paul Getty Museum, 1991.

Bennett, Stuart. *How to Buy Photographs.* Oxford: Phaidon, 1987.

Blodgett, Richard. *Photographs: A Collector's Guide.* New York: Ballantine Books, 1979.

Brown, Leslie, David Coleman, and Stephan F. Florian Jost. *Re-Collecting: Photographs from the Harry Ransom Humanities Research Center.* Austin, TX: Harry Ransom Humanities Research Center, 1997.

Castle, Peter. *Collecting and Valuing Old Photographs.* London: Garnstone Press, 1973.

Coleman, A. D. "Photography as Material Culture: What are the Vintage Years?" *Art on Paper* 5 (November-December 2000): 56–60.

Crawford, William. *The Keepers of Light: A History & Working Guide to Early Photographic Processes.* Dobbs Ferry, NY: Morgan & Morgan, 1979.

Dating Old Photographs, 1840–1929. Toronto, Ontario: Family Chronicle, 2000.

Dykstra, Jean. "In the Vernacular," *Art & Auction* 21 (September 21–October 4, 1998): 49.

Foresta, Merry A., and Jeana Kae Foley. *At First Sight: Photography and the Smithsonian.* Washington, DC: Smithsonian Books, 2003.

Frisch, Karen. *Unlocking the Secrets in Old Photographs.* Salt Lake City, UT: Ancestry, 1990.

Gilbert, George. *Collecting Photographica: The Images and Equipment of the First Hundred Years of Photography.* New York: Hawthorn Books, 1976.

Goranin, Näkki. *American Photobooth.* New York: W. W. Norton & Company, 2008.

Haller, Margaret. *Collecting Old Photographs.* New York: Arco Publishing Company, 1978.

Hannavy, John. *Case Histories: The Packaging and Presentation of the Photographic Portrait in Victorian Britain 1840–1875.* Suffolk, UK: Antique Collectors' Club, 2005.

Ibson, John. *Picturing Men: A Century of Male Relationships in Everyday American Photography.* Washington, DC: Smithsonian Institution Press, 2002.

Johnson, Robert Flynn, and William Boyd. *Anonymous: Enigmatic Images from Unknown Photographers.* New York: Thames & Hudson, 2004.

Kenny, Adele. *Photographic Cases: Victorian Design Sources, 1840–1870.* Atglen, PA: Schiffer Pub., 2001.

Klamkin, Charles. *Photographica: A Guide to the Value of Historic Cameras and Images.* New York: Funk and Wagnall's, 1978.

Mace, O. Henry. *Collector's Guide to Early Photographs.* Radnor, PA: Wallace and Homestead Book Company, 1990.

Madigan, Mary. *Prints & Photographs: Understanding, Appreciating, Collecting.* New York: Billboard Publications, 1983.

Martin, Elizabeth. *Collecting and Preserving Old Photographs.* London: Collins, 1988.

Meyers, Laura. "Galleries Focus on Vernacular Photos with Eye on Profit, Sales," *Art Business News* 26 (March 1999): 12.

————. "Modern-day Collectors Snap up Vintage Travel Photographs," *Art Business News* 27 (November 2000): 8, 92–93.

Nickell, Joe. *Camera Clues: A Handbook for Photographic Investigation.* Lexington, KY: University Press of Kentucky, 1994.

"Photo Fairs Multiply," *Art on Paper* 3 (January-February 1999): 20–21.

Pine, Gail, and Jackie Woods. "The Art of the Anonymous: Special Feature on Collecting Vernacular Photography," *Black & White Magazine* 38 (August 2005): 32–41.

Reilly, James M. *Care and Identification of 19th-Century Photographic Prints.* Rochester, NY: Eastman Kodak Company, 1986.

Schaffner, Ingrid, et al. *Deep Storage: Collecting, Storing, and Archiving in Art.* Munich and New York: Prestel, 1998.

Schneider, Stuart L. *Collecting Picture and Photo Frames.* Atglen, PA: Schiffer Pub., 1998.

Schonauer, David. "Triumph of Vernacular," *American Photo* 11 (September-October 2000): 20.

Siegel, Alan, et al. *One Man's Eye: Photographs from the Alan Siegel Collection.* New York: Abrams, 2000.

Siegel, Alan. "Alan Siegel on Building an Eclectic Collection of Photographs," *Art on Paper* 7 (November-December 2002): 109.

Smith, Rosalind. "Rodger Kingston's Forgotten Photographs: A Collector of the Not-So-Famous Image Makers," *Shutterbug* 26, no. 10 (August 1997): 74–75, 80.

Taylor, Maureen Alice. *More Dating Old Photographs, 1840–1929.* Toronto, Ontario: Family Chronicle, 2004.

Vanderbilt, Paul. *Evaluating Historical Photographs: A Personal Perspective.* Nashville: American Association for State and Local History, 1979.

Warner, Glen. *Building a Print Collection: A Guide to Buying Original Prints and Photographs.* New York: Van Nostrand Reinhold, 1981.

Weinstein, Robert. *Collection, Use, and Care of Historical Photographs.* Nashville: American Association for State and Local History, 1977.

Welling, William. *Collectors' Guide to Nineteenth-Century Photographs.* New York: Collier Books, 1976.

Witkin, Lee. *The Photograph Collector's Guide.* Boston: New York Graphic Society, 1979.

Zanes, Warren. "The Flea Market Museum," *Afterimage* 28 (September-October 2000): 13.

Vernacular Pictures and Practices—A Selected List

Anthropology and Photography

Banta, Melissa, Curtis M. Hinsley, and Joan Kathryn O'Donnell. *From Site to Sight: Anthropology, Photography, and the Power of Imagery.* Cambridge: Peabody Museum Press, 1986.

Chalfen, Richard M. *Celebrating Life with Photographs: An Approach from Visual Anthropology.* Berkeley: R. M. Chalfen, 1987.

Edwards, Elizabeth. *Raw Histories: Photographs, Anthropology and Museums.* Oxford: Berg, 2001.

————. *Anthropology and Photography, 1860–1920.* New Haven: Yale University Press, 1992.

Hight, Eleanor M., and Gary D. Sampson, eds. *Colonialist Photography: Imag(in)Ing Race and Place.* London: Routledge, 2002.

Lee, Anthony W. *A Shoe-Maker's Story: Being Chiefly About French Canadian Immigrants, Enterprising Photographers, Rascal Yankees, and Chinese Cobblers in a Nineteenth-Century Factory Town.* Princeton: Princeton University Press, 2008.

————. *Picturing Chinatown: Art and Orientalism in San Francisco.* Berkeley: University of California Press, 2001.

Pinney, Christopher. *Camera Indica: The Social Life of Indian Photographs.* London: Reaktion Books, 1997.

Pinney, Christopher, and Nicolas Peterson, eds. *Photography's Other Histories.* Durham: Duke University Press, 2003.

Crime Scene and Other Photographic "Evidence"

Gibson, Ross. "Where the Darkness Loiters," *History of Photography* 24, no. 3 (Autumn 2000): 251–254.

Hannigan, William. *New York Noir: Crime Photographs from the Daily News Archive.* New York: Rizzoli, 1999.

Michaelson, Mark, and Steven Kasher. *Least Wanted: A Century of*

American Mugshots. New York and Göttingen, Germany: Steven Kasher Gallery and Steidl, 2006.

Novakov, Anna. "Police Pictures: The Photograph as Evidence," *Art Press* 233 (March 1998): 74–76.

Panzer, Mary. "Does Crime Pay?" *Archives of American Art Journal* 37 (1997): 17–24.

Parry, Eugenia. *Crime Album Stories, Paris 1866–1902.* Zurich: Scalo, 2000.

Phillips, Sandra. *Police Pictures: The Photograph as Evidence.* San Francisco: Chronicle Books, 1997.

Pountney, Harold. *Police Photography.* New York: Elsevier, 1971.

Sante, Luc. *Evidence.* New York: Farrar, Straus and Giroux, 1992.

Sekula, Allan. "The Body and the Archive." In *The Contest of Meaning: Critical Histories of Photography*, edited by Richard Bolton. Cambridge: MIT Press, 1989.

Tagg, John. *The Burden of Representation: Essays on Photographies and Histories.* Minneapolis: University of Minnesota Press, 1988.

Erotic Photography

Bright, Deborah. *The Passionate Camera: Photography and Bodies of Desire.* London: Routledge, 1998.

Crombie, Isobel. "Private Pleasures: An Example of French Photographic Erotica," *Art Bulletin of Victoria* 37 (1996): 47–51.

Dennis, Kelly. "Ethno-pornography: Veiling the Dark Continent," *History of Photography* 18 (Spring 1994): 22–28.

Ellenzweig, Allen. *The Homoerotic Photograph: Male Images from Durieu/Delacroix to Mapplethorpe.* New York: Columbia University Press, 1992.

Gabor, Mark. *The Illustrated History of Girlie Magazines: From National Police Gazette to the Present.* New York: Harmony Books, 1984.

Institute for Sex Research, Jeffrey A. Wolin, Betsy Stirratt, Carol Squiers, and Jennifer P. Yamashiro. *Peek: Photographs from the Kinsey Institute.* Santa Fe, NM: Arena Editions, 2000.

Köhler, Michael. "Nude/Photo: The History of the Genre as an Exploration of a Fascination and its Partial Suppression," *European Photography* 3 (July-September, 1982): 4–31.

Lee Phillips, Donna. *Eros and Photography: An Explanation of Sexual Imagery and Photographic Practice.* San Francisco: Camerawork/ NFS Press, 1977.

Mavor, Carol. *Pleasures Taken: Performances of Sexuality and Loss in Victorian Photographs.* Durham: Duke University Press, 1995.

Metz, Christian. "Photography and Fetish," *October* 34 (Fall 1985): 81–90.

Nazarieff, Serge. *Early Erotic Photography.* Köln: Benedikt Taschen, 1993.

Ovenden, Graham, and Peter Mendes. *Victorian Erotic Photography.* New York: St. Martin's Press, 1973.

Pearsons, Jennifer. "Erotic and Pornographic Photography: Selected Bibliography," *History of Photography* 18 (Spring 1994): 47–49.

Peterson, Jim. *Playboy 50 Years: The Photographs.* San Francisco: Chronicle Books, 2003.

Romer, Grant. *Die Erotische Daguerreotype: Sammlung Uwe Scheid.* Weingarten: Kunstverlag Weingarter, 1990.

Weiermair, Peter. *The Hidden Image: Photographs of the Male Nude in the Nineteenth and Twentieth Centuries.* Cambridge: MIT Press, 1988.

Family Albums and Other Photographic Albums

Di Bello, Patrizia. *Women's Albums and Photography in Victorian England: Ladies, Mothers and Flirts.* Aldershot, UK: Ashgate, 2007.

Kotkin, Amy. "The Family Photo Album as a Folklore," *Exposure* 16 (March 1978): 4–8.

Langford, Martha. *Suspended Conversations: The Afterlife of Memory in Photographic Albums.* Montreal: McGill-Queen's University Press, 2001.

Levine, Barbara, and Kirsten M. Jensen. *Around the World: The Grand Tour in Photo Albums.* New York: Princeton Architectural Press, 2007.

Levine, Barbara, and Stephanie Snyder. *Snapshot Chronicles: Inventing the American Photo Album.* New York: Princeton Architectural Press, 2006.

Lowing, Robert. "The Family Album: A Feminist Perspective," *Exposure* 32 (1999): 19–27.

Miller, J. MacNeill. "The Impersonal Album: Chronicling Life in the Digital Age," *Afterimage* 35, no. 2 (September-October 2007): 9–12.

Motz, Marilyn. "Visual Autobiography: Photograph Albums of Turn-of-the-Century Midwestern Women," *American Quarterly* 41 (March 1989): 63–92.

Nordström, Alison. "Travel Albums." In *Original Sources: Art and Archives at the Center for Creative Photography*, edited by Amy Rule and Nancy Solomon; research assistance by Leon Zimlich.

Tucson, AZ: Center for Creative Photography, University of Arizona, 2002.

Siegel, Elizabeth. "'Miss Domestic' and 'Miss Enterprise': *Or, How to Keep a Photograph Album*." In *The Scrapbook in American Life*, edited by Susan Tucker, Katherine Ott, and Patricia P. Buckler. Philadelphia: Temple University Press, 2006.

———. "Galleries of Friendship and Fame: The History of Nineteenth-Century American Photograph Albums." Ph.D. diss., University of Chicago, 2003.

Silber, Mark. *The Family Album: Photographs of the 1890s and 1900s*. Boston: David R. Godine, 1973.

Stokes, Philip. "The Family Photograph Album: So Great a Cloud of Witnesses." In *The Portrait in Photography*, edited by Graham Clarke. New York: Reaktion Books, 1992.

Family Photographs

Aries, Philippe. "Pictures of the Family." In *Centuries of Childhood: A Social History of Family Life*, translated by Robert Baldick. New York: Vintage Press, 1962.

Burns, Stanley B., and Elizabeth A. Burns. *Sleeping Beauty II: Grief, Bereavement and the Family in Memorial Photography, American & European Traditions*. New York: Burns Archive Press, 2002.

Hattersley, Ralph. "Family Photography as a Sacrament," *Popular Photography* 68 (June 1971): 106–109.

Hirsch, Julia. *Family Photographs: Content, Meaning and Effect*. New York: Oxford University Press, 1981.

Hirsch, Marianne, ed. *The Familial Gaze*. Hanover, NH: Dartmouth College, 1999.

Kuhn, Annette. *Family Secrets: Acts of Memory and Imagination*. London: Verso, 1995.

Lesy, Michael. *Time Frames: The Meaning of Family Pictures*. New York: Pantheon Books, 1980.

Ohrn, Karin. "The Photo Flow of Family Life: A Family Photograph Collection," *Folklore Forum* 13 (1975): 27–36.

Pols, Robert. *Family Photographs, 1860–1945*. Richmond, Surrey: Public Record Office, 2002.

Reiakvam, Oddlaug. "Reframing the Family Photograph," *Journal of Popular Culture* 26 (Spring 1993): 3–63.

Silber, Mark. *The Family Album: Photographs of the 1890s and 1900s, by Gilbert Wight Tilton & Fred W. Record*. Boston: David R. Godine, 1973.

Slater, Dan. "Domestic Photography and Digital Culture." In *The Photographic Image in Digital Culture*, edited by Martin Lister. New York & London: Routledge, 1995.

Spence, Jo, and Patricia Holland, eds. *Family Snaps: The Meanings of Domestic Photography*. London: Virago, 1991.

Stricherz, Guy. *Americans in Kodachrome 1945–1965*. Santa Fe, NM: Twin Palms Publishers, 2002.

Tufte, Virginia, and Barbara Myerhoff. *Changing Images of the Family*. New Haven: Yale University Press, 1979.

Wills, Deborah. *Picturing Us: African American Identity in Photography*. New York: New Press, 1994.

Williams, Val. *Who's Looking at the Family?* London: Barbican Art Gallery, 1999.

———. "Cultural Sniping: The Art of Transgression and Family Secrets," *Creative Camera* 335 (August-September 1995): 37–38.

The Found Image

Bentley, Kevin. *Sailor: Vintage Photos of a Masculine Icon*. San Francisco: Council Oak Books, 2000.

Bitner, Jason. *Found Polaroids*. Ann Arbor, MI: Quack!Media, 2006.

———. *Laporte, Indiana*. New York: Princeton Architectural Press, 2006.

DeLano, Sharon, and Roger Handy. *Summer Vacation/Found Photographs*. Santa Barbara, CA: T. Adler Books, 2000.

Frizot, Michel, and Cédric de Veigy. *Photo Trouvée*. Paris: Phaidon, 2006.

Lost & Found in America: From the Collection of Lenny Gottlieb. Stockport, UK: Dewi Lewis, 2004.

Nocito, James. *Found Lives: A Collection of Found Photographs*. Layton, UT: Gibbs Smith, 1998.

Phoenix, Charles. *Southern Californialand: Mid-Century Culture in Kodachrome*. Santa Monica, CA: Angel City Press, 2004.

West, Nancy Martha. "Telling Time: Found Photographs and the Stories They Inspire." In *Now Is Then: Snapshots from the Maresca Collection*, by Marvin Heiferman, Geoffrey Batchen, and Nancy Martha West. New York: Princeton Architectural Press, 2008.

Medical and Scientific Photography

Art Journal 62, no. 3 (Fall 2003). [Issue on photography and the paranormal.]

Burns, Stanley B. *Early Medical Photography in America 1839–1883.* New York: Burns Archive, 1983.

———. *A Morning's Work: Medical Photographs from the Burns Archive & Collection, 1843–1939.* Santa Fe, NM: Twin Palms Publishers, 1998.

Dermer, Rachelle A. "Joel-Peter Witkin and Dr. Stanley B. Burns: A Language of Body Parts." *History of Photography* 23 no. 3 (Autumn 1999): 245–253. [Issue on medicine and photography.]

Glenner, Richard A., Audrey B. Davis, and Stanley B. Burns. *The American Dentist: A Pictorial History with a Presentation of Early Dental Photography in America.* Missoula, MT: Pictorial Histories Pub. Co., 1990.

Hamilton, Peter, and Roger Hargreaves. *The Beautiful and the Damned: The Creation of Identity in Nineteenth Century Photography.* Aldershot, UK: Lund Humphries, 2001.

Marable, Darwin. "Photography and Human Behaviour in the Nineteenth Century," *History of Photography* 9 (April-June 1985): 141–147.

Newman, Kathy. "Wounds and Wounding in the American Civil War: A Visual History," *Yale Journal of Criticism* 6 (1992): 63–86.

O'Connor, Erin. "Camera Medica: Towards a Morbid History of Photography," *History of Photography* 23, no. 3 (Autumn 1999): 232–244.

Thomas, Ann, and Marta Braun. *Beauty of Another Order: Photography in Science.* New Haven: Yale University Press in Association with the National Gallery of Canada, Ottawa, 1997.

Photographic Postcards

Artes de Mexico 48 (2000). [Issue on "Postcards: The Power of Fleeting Memories."]

Bogdan, Robert, and Todd Weseloh. *Real Photo Postcard Guide: The People's Photography.* Syracuse, NY: Syracuse University Press, 2006.

Chien, David. *About 85 Years Ago: Photo Postcards from America 1907–1920.* Niwot, CO: Roberts Rinehart Publishing, 1997.

Fraser, John. "Propaganda on the Picture Postcard," *Oxford Art Journal* 3 (October 1980): 39–47.

Klich, Lynda. "Little Women: The Female Nude in the Golden Age of Picture Postcards," *Visual Resources* 17, no. 4 (2001): 435–438.

McCulloch, Lou W. *Card Photographs: A Guide to Their History and Value.* Exton, PA: Schiffer Pub., 1981.

Morgan, Hal. *Prairie Fires and Paper Moons: The American Photographic Postcard, 1900–1920.* Boston: David R. Godine, 1981.

———. *Big Time: American Tall-Tale Postcards.* New York: St. Martin's Press, 1981.

Meikle, Jeffery L. "A Paper Atlantis: Postcards, Mass Art, and the American Scene," *Journal of Design History* 13 (2000): 267–286.

Morphet, Richard. *Wish You Were Here: The History of the Picture Postcard.* Hempstead, NY: Emily Lowe Art Gallery, Hofstra University, 1974.

Rubin, Cynthia, and Morgan Williams. *Larger than Life: The American Tall-Tale Postcard, 1905–1915.* New York: Abbeville Press, 1990.

Ruby, Jay. "Images of Rural America: View Photographs and Picture Postcards," *History of Photography* 12 (October-December 1988): 327–343.

Schur, Naomi. "'Cartes Postales': Representing Paris 1900," *Critical Inquiry* 18, no. 2 (Winter 1992): 188–244.

Sigel, Lisa Z. "Filth in the Wrong People's Hands: Postcards and the Expansion of Pornography in Britain and the Atlantic World, 1880–1914," *Journal of Social History* 33, no. 4 (Summer 2000): 859–885.

Snow, Rachel. "Postscript to a Postcard," *Afterimage* 29 (May-June 2002): 6–7.

Thiriez, Regine. "Imperial China in Postcards," *Orientations* 35, no. 5 (June 2004): 46–51.

Tulcensky, Harvey, Laetitia Wolff, and Todd Alden. *Real Photo Postcards: Unbelievable Images from the Collection of Harvey Tulcensky.* New York: Princeton Architectural Press, 2005.

Vaule, Rosamond B. *As We Were: American Photographic Postcards, 1905–1930.* Boston: David R. Godine, 2004.

Welsch, Roger. *Tall-Tale Postcards: A Pictorial History.* New Jersey: A. S. Barnes and Company, 1976.

The Photographic Portrait

Burns, Stanley. *Forgotten Marriage: The Painted Tintype & The Decorative Frame, 1860–1910: A Lost Chapter in American Portraiture.* New York: Burns Press, 1995.

Foresta, Merry A., and John Wood. *Secrets of the Dark Chamber: The*

Art of the American Daguerreotype. Washington, DC: National Museum of American Art, Smithsonian Institution Press, 1995.

Hannavy, John. *Case Histories: The Packaging and Presentation of the Photographic Portrait in Victorian Britain 1840–1875.* Woodbridge, Suffolk: Antique Collectors' Club, 2005.

Henisch, Heinz K., and Bridget A. Henisch. *The Painted Photograph, 1839–1914: Origins, Techniques, Aspirations.* University Park, PA: Pennsylvania State University Press, 1996.

McCauley, Elizabeth Anne. *Industrial Madness: Commercial Photography in Paris, 1848–1871.* New Haven: Yale University Press, 1994.

————. *A.A.E. Disdéri and the Carte de Visite Portrait Photograph.* New Haven: Yale University Press, 1985.

Ruby, Jay. *Secure the Shadow: Death and Photography in America.* Cambridge: MIT Press, 1995.

Severa, Joan L. *My Likeness Taken: Daguerreian Portraits in America.* Kent, OH: Kent State University Press, 2005.

————. *Dressed for the Photographer: Ordinary Americans and Fashion, 1840–1900.* Kent, OH: Kent State University Press, 1995.

Wyman, James B., et al. "From the Background to the Foreground: The Photo Backdrop and Cultural Expression," *Afterimage* 24, no. 5 (March-April 1997). [Issue on the photo backdrop.]

The Snapshot and Popular Photography

The American Snapshot: An Exhibition of the Folk Art of the Camera. New York: Museum of Modern Art, 1944.

Chalfen, Richard. *Snapshot Versions of Life: Explorations of Home-Made Photography.* Bowling Green, IN: Bowling Green State University Popular Press, 1987.

Coe, Brian, and Paul Gates. *The Snapshot Photograph: The Rise of Popular Photography, 1888–1939.* London: Ash & Grant, 1977.

Collins, Douglas. *The Story of Kodak.* New York: Abrams, 1990.

Doris, David. "'It's the Truth, it's actual . . .': Kodak picture spots at Walt Disney World," *Visual Resources* 14 (1998): 321–338.

Drugstore Photographs: Snapshots from the Collections of Christopher Rauschenberg and Terry Toedhemeier. New York: Pair o' Dice Press, 1976.

Ford, Colin, ed. *The Story of Popular Photography.* North Pomfret, VT: Trafalgar Square Publishing, 1989.

Ford, Colin, and Karl Steinorth, eds. *You Press the Button, We Do the Rest.* London: Dirk Nishen Publishing, 1988.

Graves, Ken, and Mitchell Payne. *American Snapshots.* Oakland, CA: Scrimshaw Press, 1977.

Green, Jonathan. *The Snap-Shot.* Millerton, NY: Aperture, 1974.

Greenough, Sarah, Dianna Waggoner, Sarah Kennel, and Matthew S. Witkovsky. *The Art of the American Snapshot, 1888–1978.* Princeton, NJ: Princeton University Press, 2007.

Heiferman, Marvin, Geoffrey Batchen, and Nancy Martha West. *Now Is Then: Snapshots from the Maresca Collection.* New York: Princeton Architectural Press, 2008.

Kenyon, Dave. *Inside Amateur Photography.* London: B. T. Batsford Ltd., 1992.

King, Graham. *Snaps as Art: A Brief Study of the Photographic Snap.* London: Pimlico Press, 1978.

————. *Say "Cheese"! Looking at Snapshots in a New Way.* New York: Dodd, Mead & Co., 1984.

Mensel, Robert. "'Kodakers Lying in Wait': Amateur Photography and the Right of Privacy in New York, 1885–1915," *American Quarterly* 43 (March 1991): 24–45.

Nickel, Douglas R. *Snapshots: The Photography of Everyday Life, 1888 to the Present.* San Francisco: San Francisco Museum of Modern Art, 1998.

————. "Roland Barthes and the Snapshot," *History of Photography* 24, no. 3 (Autumn 2000): 232–235.

Skrein, Christian, and Carl Aigner. *Snapshots: The Eye of the Century.* Ostfildern: Hatje Cantz, 2004.

Smith, Joel. "Roll Over: The Snapshot's Museum Afterlife," *Afterimage* 29, no. 2 (September–October 2001): 8–11.

"The Snapshot," *Aperture* 19 (1974). [Special issue.]

The Stereoscopic Image

Darrah, William Culp. *Stereo Views: A History of Stereographs in America and Their Collection.* Gettysburg, PA: Times and News Publishing Company, 1964.

————. "Stereographs: A Neglected Source of the History of Photography." In *One Hundred Years of Photographic History,* edited by Van Deren Coke. Albuquerque, NM: University of New Mexico Press, 1975.

————. *The World of Stereographs.* Gettysburg, PA: Darrah, 1977.

Earle, Edward W., Howard Saul Becker, Thomas W. Southall, and Harvey Green. *Points of View, the Stereograph in America: A Cul-*

tural History. Rochester, NY: Visual Studies Workshop Press, 1979.

Hamilton, George E. *Oliver Wendell Holmes: His Pioneer Stereoscope and the Later Industry.* New York: Newcomen Society of North America, 1949.

Jones, John. *Wonders of the Stereoscope.* London: J. Cape, 1976.

Joseph, Steven. "Wheatstone's Double Vision," *History of Photography* 8 (October-December 1984): 329–332.

McKay, H. C. *Three-Dimensional Photography: Principles of Stereoscopy.* New York: American Photography Book Department, 1953.

Silverman, Robert. "The Stereoscope and Photographic Depiction in the 19th century," *Technology and Culture* 34 (October 1993): 729–756.

Waldsmith, John S. *Stereo Views: An Illustrated History & Price Guide.* Iola, WI: Krause Publications, 2002.

West, Nancy. "Fantasy, Photography, and the Marketplace: Oliver Wendell Holmes and the Stereoscope," *Nineteenth-Century Contexts* 19 (1996): 231–258.

Wing, Paul. *Stereoscopes: The First One Hundred Years.* Nashua, NH: Transition Publishing, 1996.

Zimmerman, Logen. "The 'Original' J. A. Williams," *Stereo World* 31, no. 2 (September-October 2005): 28–33.

————. "Bryant Bradley's 'Mount Desert Scenery'," *Stereo World* 32, no. 2 (September-October 2006): 28–33.

Zone, Ray. *Stereoscopic Cinema & the Origins of 3-D Film, 1838–1952.* Lexington, KY: The University Press of Kentucky, 2007.

CONTRIBUTORS

Ross Barrett is a Ph.D. candidate in art history at Boston University, specializing in American art, architecture, and visual culture of the nineteenth and twentieth centuries. He is the 2006–2008 Wyeth Fellow in American Art at the Center for Advanced Study in the Visual Arts (CASVA), and has previously held fellowships from the American Council of Learned Societies and the American Antiquarian Society. He was the 2002–2005 Warren G. Adelson Curatorial Fellow in American Art at Boston University. Barrett has published articles in *Prospects: An Annual of American Cultural Studies*, *The Book*, and *Winterthur Portfolio*. His research has focused on the interrelationships of painting and popular print imagery, the pictorial representation of violence, landscape aesthetics and real estate speculation, popular depictions of workers and working-class culture, and the visual culture of business and corporations. He has taught courses in American and modern art at Syracuse and in Boston.

Stacey McCarroll Cutshaw was Director & Curator of the Boston University Art Gallery from 2002 to 2007, where she co-curated, with Ross Barrett, *In the Vernacular: Everyday Photographs from the Rodger Kingston Collection* (2004–2005) and organized the accompanying two-day academic conference on vernacular photography, *Vernacular Reframed*. A specialist in twentieth-century American photography and visual culture, Cutshaw was the curator and author of the Boston University Art Gallery exhibition and publication, *California Dreamin':*

Camera Clubs and the Pictorial Photography Tradition (2004), and curator of *Offspring: Representations of Children in Contemporary Visual Culture* (2006). She has published book reviews in *Afterimage* and *Signs: Journal of Women in Culture and Society*, as well as short essays and catalog entries in *The Chronicle Review* and *The Encyclopedia of Twentieth Century Photography*. Cutshaw has taught courses in modern and contemporary art, the history of photography, and museum studies in California and Massachusetts since 1994.

Professor Bernard L. Herman is Chair and Edward F. and Elizabeth Goodman Rosenberg Professor of Art History at the University of Delaware. He co-founded and directed the Center for Material Culture Studies and co-founded the Center for Historic Architecture and Design. His courses include research and reading seminars on material culture, vernacular architecture, folk and ethnic arts, historic landscapes, and eighteenth-century American and British urbanism. His books include *Town House: Architecture and Experience in the Early American City, 1780–1830* (2005), *Everyday Architecture of The Mid-Atlantic* (1997), *The Stolen House* (1992), *A Land and Life Remembered: Americo-Liberian Folk Architecture* (1989) with Svend Holsoe and Max Belcher, and *Architecture and Rural Life in Central Delaware, 1700–1900* (1987). His forthcoming books are *Quilt Spaces* and *The First-Period Houses of the Delaware Valley from the Falls at Trenton to the Capes of Delaware, 1675–1740*.

DAILE KAPLAN is vice president and director of photographs at Swann Galleries, Inc., New York City's oldest specialty auction house. A former artist-photographer, she is an auctioneer, author, and curator who is photographs expert on the nationally acclaimed television program "Antiques Roadshow." Kaplan curated the traveling exhibition about vernacular photography *Pop Photographica, Photography's Objects in Everyday Life* for the Art Gallery of Ontario, and wrote the principal catalogue essay. Recently she contributed essays to *The Education of a Photographer* (2006) and *The Focal Encyclopedia of Photography* (2007). A noted scholar of the pre-eminent American photojournalist, Lewis W. Hine, she has written two books about him, published by the Abbeville and Smithsonian Institution Press. She also authored *Premiere Nudes* (2001), a monograph about the Roaring Twenties photographer Albert Arthur Allen. Kaplan is on the Board of Directors of the Appraisers Association of America, Alexia Foundation, Fifty Crows, and the Palm Beach Photographic Centre.

RODGER KINGSTON has collected images by unknown photographers for over thirty years, inadvertently building a case for a new vernacular history of photography. An established photographer himself, Kingston has embraced collecting with the same passion that informs his own work: the urge to elevate a quotidian or populist point of view. An expert on Walker Evans, Kingston wrote the book *Walker Evans in Print: An Illustrated Bibliography* (1995). He has exhibited his photographic work extensively throughout the United States, including the exhibition *Along the Right of Way: Landscapes from a Train* at the Fuller Museum of Art, Brockton, Massachusetts, in 2002. His 1998 exhibition, *Fifty Years on the Mangrove Coast: Photographs by Walker Evans and Rodger Kingston*, traveled to five museums over the course of two years. His work is in numerous collections, including the Boston Museum of Fine Arts, The National Gallery of American Art, and the Fogg Art Museum.

BOSTON UNIVERSITY

President: Robert A. Brown

Provost: David K. Campbell

COLLEGE OF ARTS AND SCIENCES

Dean: Virginia Sapiro

Chair, Art History Department: Fred S. Kleiner

Associate Chair, Art History Department: Michael Zell

COLLEGE OF FINE ARTS

Dean, ad interim: Walt C. Meissner

Director, School of Visual Arts: Lynne D. Allen

BOSTON UNIVERSITY ART GALLERY

at the Stone Gallery

855 Commonwealth Avenue

Boston, Massachusetts 02215

617-353-3329

www.bu.edu/art

Director, ad interim: Marc Mitchell

Senior Security Assistant: Evelyn Cohen

Gallery Assistants: Kaia Balcos, Michael Garguilo, Rebecca Hathaway,
Molly Hopper, Gina Iacobelli, Samantha Kattan, MacKenzie Klump,
Karen Ann Myers, Ron Nadarski, Natania Remba, Leann Rittenbaum,
Lana Sloutsky, and Alison Yuhas.

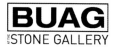

All images reproduced courtesy the
Rodger Kingston Collection unless otherwise noted.

Typeset and printed at The Stinehour Press, Lunenburg, Vermont

Binding by Acme Bookbinding, Charlestown, Massachusetts

Design by Paul Hoffmann